The Book of Lech Wałęsa

Introduced by Neal Ascherson

Simon and Schuster
New York

Published by arrangement with OY International Business Service
Limited, Helsinki, Finland, 1982.

Walesa first published by Wydawnictwo Morskie, Gdańsk, 1981

Published by Simon & Schuster,
A Division of Gulf & Western Corporation
Simon & Schuster Building
Rockefeller Center
1230 Avenue of the Americas
New York, New York 10020
SIMON AND SCHUSTER and colophon are trademarks of Simon & Schuster

Manufactured in the United States of America
1 2 3 4 5 6 7 8 9 10
1 2 3 4 5 6 7 8 9 10 Pbk.

Library of Congress Cataloging in Publication Data
ISBN 0–671–45684–9
ISBN 0–671–45683–0 Pbk.

Contents

6   Contents

Introduction

Lech Wałęsa, an electrician, became for sixteen months one of the most famous men in the world. He led the strike which began at the Lenin shipyard in Gdańsk on 14 August 1980. He signed the Gdańsk agreement on 31 August which announced the triumph of the strike and the emergence of the 'independent, self-managing trade union Solidarity', and as the union spread throughout Poland, eventually acquiring some nine and a half million members, there was no question that anyone but Wałęsa should be the first chairman of its provisional executive. The union's first national congress in September and October the following year re-elected him chairman, against the candidature of several more militant rivals, and he was still Solidarity's leader on 13 December 1981, when General Wojciech Jaruzelski imposed martial law, suspended Solidarity and arrested thousands of its officials and activists. Wałęsa's face, during those months, appeared on magazine covers and television screens in every country. The teleprinters relayed across the globe every comment he cared to make. Young men in France and Germany, the United States and Britain, grew imitations of his long 'Sarmatian' moustache. Next to the Pope, he was the most celebrated Pole alive.

I forget exactly when I first saw him. It was during the August strike at Gdańsk, when we in the world press had only just learned to spell his name. The negotiations with the government were nearing their climax. Perhaps I first saw him in one of those sudden eddies of the crowd, as he tore across the shipyard scribbling autographs and scattering little coloured cards of the Madonna of Częstochowa. It was hard to get a proper look; he seemed always to rush, never to walk, and the press of men in drab overalls around him constantly hid his short figure from view. My first chance to study him properly came during a break in the talks, a few days later. The door of the strike praesidium room had been left unguarded, and I strolled in. Wałęsa was sitting on a chair, with a little girl in a cheap tartan dress on his knee (one of his many children), talking to a group of his advisers. They were standing, frowning down at him, raising difficulties. As he glanced up at them, I was struck by the foxiness of his appearance: the long narrow nose, the sharp russet eyes, the sense of quickness and cunning which this look and his staccato sentences put across.

As the strike went on, the nature of his hold over the movement turned out to be more complicated than it had at first seemed. Wałęsa was at once more and less than a demagogue. He was a consummate, even outrageous manipulator; I once saw him put three mutually exclusive resolutions to the main strike committee within a few minutes and have them all accepted by acclaim. He could be dictatorial, often snatching the microphone from a colleague who was in mid-sentence. He was certainly a born trouble-maker, but a trouble-maker who lusted after compromise rather than extremes. As his whole career in those sixteen months showed, Wałęsa adored the actual business of negotiating: the shatteringly hard opening position, the leaving of doors ajar, the gradual trading-off in hard talk sessions until both sides could shake hands with pride on a gleaming new settlement. Many of his colleagues entirely lacked this taste. They wanted to leave the negotiating table with all their demands won and no concessions made. But Wałęsa preferred a genuine joint settlement, talked out until opponents had become accomplices. '*Polak z Polakiem musi się dogadać*' – 'Pole must talk things out with Pole', he used endlessly to repeat.

'Charisma' is not a useful word. As Maria Janion says in this book, the electrician did somehow communicate electricity, send currents circuiting between him and his mass audiences. But it was the ambiguity of his relation to the crowd which struck me most at Gdańsk. On the one hand the workers worshipped Wałęsa; they cheered him, chanted his name, brought him little presents, reached out to touch him as he passed. And yet, on the other hand, this worship was entirely provisional. They were well aware that Wałęsa was fallible and vain, and when he put a foot wrong they would noisily oppose him. Is it possible to combine passionate loyalty and affectionate contempt? They were combined at Gdańsk. It was just because the workers saw that 'Leszek' was one of them – and no better than they – that they managed to square that psychological circle.

For he really was a workers' tribune, which is more than a spellbinder. The influence of Jimmy Reid, a leader of the great workers' take-over at Upper Clyde shipyards in 1971, was as much to do with his talents as a comic as with his socialist eloquence. Wałęsa dominated the Gdańsk strike not through oratory but by something much more proletarian: patter. He made people laugh, seemed a chancer, a card. And he conveyed the hint that he was more at home with foul means than fair. In Glasgow and Gdańsk, where 'they' frame the Queensberry Rules so that nobody at the bottom of the heap can win by them, a touch of lawlessness in a leader is well taken.

He seemed to bask in publicity. But in reality he was evasive with journalists, almost never dropping his guard or allowing himself to enter a serious conversation (an exception that proves the rule is the interview with Marzena and Tadeusz Woźniak in this book, who lured Wałęsa further than he meant to go). Behind the bonhomie, he probably despised the mass media, enjoying their flattery but clever enough to give as little as he could in return. Immensely proud of his power as the workers' spokesman, Wałęsa never mentally crossed the line which divides workers from the Establishment. Those who gave him power could take it away again. As he says here, 'I was at the bottom, and I will be at the bottom.' His vanity, which was considerable, was not really personal but an expression of pride that this electrician, pious but no better than he should be, had been chosen to perform this task. Chosen by whom? Not simply by the working class. Wałęsa's self-confidence was messianic, and he may have taken seriously the idea that it was God and his Mother who had chosen him to lead the nation out of bondage. And like many messianic figures 'called' from obscurity (Joan of Arc, Cincinnatus), he hoped to become a nobody again when his assignment was over.

The essays and tributes in this book tell us above all what Wałęsa meant to his fellow-Poles. They show us where he came from – the valiant little Land of Dobrzyń devastated by so many of Poland's political disasters, the locked and empty hut behind a birch brakᵉ where he was born, the cottage of the grandfather who also had whiskers and once hid Józef Piłsudski from the police. And they show how Polish literary culture effortlessly pervaded the subconscious of this man so impatient that he claims never to have finished a book. But in the end, this work is an extraordinary study in Polish nationalism, that intense and sealed-off culture in which industrial workers are at ease with their own classic poetry, in which the time dimension dissolves so that lines of nineteenth-century heroic drama may be the best guide to twentieth-century political crises, in which the cause of independence, Catholic belief and personal morality are compressed into a single explosive compound.

There are elements of ancestor-worship here. The bloody shirt of the insurrectionary is handed down from generation to generation. The first written expression of the Gdańsk strikes was – as Maria Janion tells us here – to pin a verse of Byron's to a cross, that verse which speaks of '... Freedom's battle once begun, Bequeathed by bleeding sire to son ...'.

To mark their peaceful intentions, the strikers left out the word 'bleeding'. But those lines also hold an important clue to Wałęsa's own personality. The most powerful of all his motives in his years of illegal struggle before 1980 was a sort of filial piety, a vow to honour the dead of the strikes of December 1970. Year after year on 16 December he made his way to the place outside the Lenin shipyard where the monument now stands, urging his comrades to bring building stones with them, and every year the little group was dispersed or arrested only to return again on the next anniversary. This obsession with the martyred dead, so much a part of the national psychology, was the source of his driving anger and his obstinacy. This young electrician is best understood, when all has been said, as a Polish Antigone.

NEAL ASCHERSON

Notes on Contributors

Lech Bądkowski is a novelist and Solidarity columnist on the Gdańsk newspaper *Dziennek Baltycki*. He acted as an adviser during the strike negotiations of August 1980.

Andrzej Drzycimski, a historian and journalist, is the author of *Poles in the Free City of Gdańsk 1920–33* (1978) and co-author of *The War Began in Westerplatte* (1979). In 1981 he received the W. Pietrzak Award, sponsored by PAX, for his writing.

Bolesław Fac, a poet and novelist, has worked in various capacities in the Gdańsk shipyard for over thirty years.

Grzegorz Fortuna is a journalist on the Gdańsk newspaper *Dziennek Baltycki*.

Maria Janion, Professor of Polish Literature at the Literary Research Institute in Warsaw and at Gdańsk University, is the author of *The Romantic Fever* (1975) and, with Maria Zmigrodzka, *Romanticism and History* (1978).

Jerzy Kołodziejski was the Governor of Gdańsk Province from 1979 until his dismissal in January 1982. He is a Professor at the Technical University at Gdańsk.

Edmund Szczesiak is known to be a journalist working in Gdańsk, but further information about him was unavailable when this book went to press.

Andrzej Wajdą, the film and theatre director and Chairman of the Polish Film Makers' Association, has since his film debut in 1955 made many internationally acclaimed feature films, including *Man of Marble* and *Man of Iron*, which was based on events in Gdańsk in August 1980 and won the Grand Prix Award at the Cannes Film Festival in 1981.

Roman Wapiński is Professor of History at Gdańsk University and the author of *Working Class Movements in Pomerania 1920–39* (1963), *National Democracy in Pomerania 1893–1939* (1980) and a biography of General Sikorski (1978).

Chronology of Modern Poland

1795. Third Partition: the Polish state extinguished.

1807–13. 'Grand Duchy of Warsaw' (Napoleon).

1815. Congress of Vienna restores the Partition.

1830–31. 'November Insurrection'.

1863–4. 'January Insurrection'.

1905–7. Revolution in Russian zone of Poland.

1914. Józef Piłsudski forms the Polish Legions.

1918. 11 November: Polish independence restored.

1920–21. Polish–Soviet War.

1926. Piłsudski takes power by *coup d'état*.

1939. German and Soviet invasion and occupation of Poland. Polish state abolished.

1944. July: Communist-dominated provisional government established in liberated areas.

August–September: Warsaw Rising.

1948–56. The Stalinist regime.

1956. June: Poznań riots.

October: Stalinism overthrown; Władysław Gomułka becomes Party leader.

1968. 'March Events': student riots repressed; purges.

1970. December: Riots in Gdańsk, Gdynia, Szczecin. Gomułka replaced by Edward Gierek.

1976. Worker strikes and riots in Radom, Warsaw.

1977. Committee for Defence of the Workers (KOR) founded.

1978. Free Trade Union Committee founded.

October: Cardinal Karol Wojtyła elected Pope.

1979. June: Pope John Paul II visits Poland.

1980. July: Strike wave begins.

14 August: Gdańsk shipyards strike.

30–31 August: Szczecin and Gdańsk agreements signed. Foundation of Solidarity.

5 September: Gierek replaced as Party leader by Stanisław Kania.

24 October: Solidarity registered as a trade union.

4–6 December: Rumours of imminent Soviet intervention.

1981. 9 February: General Wojciech Jaruzelski, Minister of Defence, becomes Prime Minister.

19 March: Police raid Solidarity strikers at Bydgoszcz.

July: Emergency congress of Polish United Workers' Party. Kania re-elected leader.

September–October: First national congress of Solidarity at Gdańsk. Lech Wałęsa elected chairman.

19 October: General Jaruzelski succeeds Kania as Party leader.

November: Negotiations between Solidarity and the government for a 'Front of National Understanding' break down.

13 December: Jaruzelski launches *coup d'état*. Poland placed under martial law; Solidarity 'suspended'; Solidarity leaders and supporters interned; Lech Wałęsa under house arrest.

Editors' Preface

The international organization Love International has awarded
Wałęsa a medal and a money prize with the citation: 'For his
contribution to the fight for human (and citizens') rights without
violence, but with love, solidarity and co-operation.' We quote
this here to stress the fact that it is as a defender of human and
civil rights, as a symbol of hope and national moral and political
revival, that Wałęsa is imprinted on the consciousness of many
millions of people.

Confidence and hope – phenomena which are linked in society's
reactions to Wałęsa's name – manifest themselves in many different
ways. Unknown people from many parts of Poland write him
letters, send him invitations to family festivals, and go to Gdańsk
to see him. People accompany him on his foreign travels, watch
their progress, participate in meetings at workshops and factories
and in stadiums, listen to his talks on the radio and on television.

While not disregarding the mass media, Wałęsa prefers direct
contact with people and feels more relaxed when addressing face
to face people whom he wants to encourage or influence. It is
not perhaps without interest that a former neighbour of Wałęsa
used to see him reading a book on crowd psychology. (Edmund
Szczesiak writes about this in his contribution to the present
volume.) Wałęsa fascinates people and this has led them to assign
him the role of Champion of the People, fighting 'Without violence,
but through love, solidarity and co-operation'.

Side by side with Pope John Paul II, Wałęsa has become one
of the most popular Poles, both in his own country and abroad. In

many of the opinion polls conducted by Western European and American publications he was selected as Man of the Year 1980. He has received various prizes and honourable mentions (all the money he receives being allotted to Solidarity). He was nominated for the Nobel Peace Prize for 1981. Several books about him have been published. He finds himself continuously in the public eye. He not only moves the hearts and minds of working people, but also awakens the enthusiasm of intellectuals thirsting for the return to basic values.

An enormous responsibility rests on Wałęsa and he never shirks it. He evokes sympathy, admiration and applause, but also resistance and dislike. He has many sympathizers, many admirers, but he does not lack enemies. Both among those well-disposed and those ill-disposed to him he has gained an enormous authority, a corollary of the values he represents. His most distinctive trait can be described as an inspired stubbornness. For Wałęsa is a stubborn man, and it is said that only stubborn people can achieve anything in life. He has already succeeded in achieving a great deal, and whatever his future fate (and whatever the methods used to research Poland's history) his place in our post-war history, as the leader of the great strike in August 1980 and as the leader of Solidarity from its inception, cannot be questioned.

Consideration of Wałęsa's public reception leads to one more observation. 'The phenomenon of Wałęsa', 'the myth of Wałęsa', are phrases that appear ever more frequently in various publications about him. The texts collected in the present volume also deal with this problem. Does he need the creation of a myth? This question is answered by one of our authors (Grzegorz Fortuna). No, Wałęsa does not need a myth, because, as he repeats frequently, he does not want to rule, or even take part in politics: he wants to serve. A myth is what a ruler, not a servant, needs. Surely we do not want to see Wałęsa glorified by a myth, because the creation of myths, in the words of the eminent scholar Mircea Eliade, proves most of all a deep discontent of man with his present situation, with what is called 'the human condition'. One can expect that in due course a perceptive sociologist will analyse 'the Wałęsa phenomenon' and will reveal the relationship between Wałęsa's past life, his personality and the social role that he has come to play.

All the essays included in the book that we now present to our readers have been written at great speed, against the deadline set by the publishers. This deadline caused some authors who might, in our opinion, have provided a lot of valuable material and some interesting assessments to refuse to participate, and resulted in others, who at first expressed interest, withdrawing later. Also, when in the middle of May 1981 we published in the press an announcement of a forthcoming book about Wałęsa, the telephone began to ring in the offices of Wydawnictwo Morskie (Maritime Publishing Co.) and letters poured in, some with words of encouragement, some critical of our enterprise. Some of the letter writers, although interested in Wałęsa, were doubtful whether it would be wise to publish a book about him when there is in Poland no biography of Józef Piłsudski* or of General Władysław Sikorski† (these were the names most often quoted). We nevertheless consider that our publication is necessary, if only because of its actuality. In passing, one might mention that, with the present crisis in the publishing and printing industries, a publisher considering any book for publication must be most careful to make the right decision. Moreover we must mention that the monographs on Piłsudski or Sikorski that are really needed would first have to be researched and written, whereas the book that we now present to our readers is not even an attempt at Wałęsa's biography. It is put together like a jigsaw puzzle, with no single thematic line. The authors' contributions are of various kinds: reportage, interviews, journalistic and sociological analyses, generalities, detailed stories etc. A book so compiled does not try for unity and objective interpretation. There are some repetitions, because different authors are dealing with the same event, the strike in August 1980, but this subject is clearly of general interest. The book does not present all the many aspects of its principal character in the round, but is rather an attempt to

---

* Józef Piłsudski (1867–1935) was the leading figure in Poland's successful struggle to regain independence in the years before 1918. He became the dominant political personality in the new state, and in 1926, exasperated by disputes with the Sejm (parliament), he took full power through a military *coup d'état*.

† General Władysław Sikorski also took part in the independence struggle before 1918. After Poland's defeat and occupation by the Germans in 1939, Sikorski formed the Polish government in exile and became its military and political leader. He was killed in an air crash at Gibraltar in 1943.

provide a quick sketch of Wałęsa, in which each author stresses those characteristics of their subject that they consider to be important – an action portrait, as the reporters Marzena and Tadeusz Woźniak have entitled the last chapter in this book, an interview with Wałęsa himself.

Chapter 1

Notes on Biography

Edmund Szczesiak

Kosztowna recognized him at once. Only she, although the whole family were watching him. It was a Sunday and they were having their tea. The TV set, as usual on Sundays and holidays, was left switched on all the time. At about five o'clock they showed a large hall, full of people; and a long table under a wall with an eagle and a cross.

'You're looking and can't see?' Kosztowna said to her husband. 'The fellow in the centre is our Wałęsiak.'

Kosztowny looked but did not see.

'He seems bigger. No, it's impossible. How could a chap from our village reach such a position?'

In the evening they showed the programme again: that long table and the wall with a cross.

'I looked again – it's definitely him. I had to look carefully because of the great moustache. Anybody who grows a beard or a set of whiskers looks different ... He was holding such a big ball-point pen ...'

Kosztowna remembers the details: the outsize ball-point pen, the rosary round his neck. At the table sat many important people, but she looked only at him. When he began to speak tears appeared in her eyes. She does not remember what he said. For her the important thing was that someone from their village spoke to the whole of Poland: someone from their Popowo.

The roneoed biographical notes tell us: 'Lech Wałęsa was born on 29 September 1943 at Popowo, in the district of Lipno.'

Where is Popowo? Anyone who looks at a map of the Włocławek region won't lose his way: the hamlet of that name is marked by a circle.

I set out from Włocławek by the road to the north, instructed that just behind the town, behind the bridge over the Vistula, another country begins. Here it is Kujawy; there, on the right bank of the river, the Land of Dobrzyń. Similar in landscape, but culturally very different regions.

'Different worlds, different people. The Kujavians are mild and quiet but the people of Dobrzyń are tough, stubborn and violent.' The local journalist traced the dividing line, quoting history and his knowledge of the countryside and of the people inhabiting the areas separated by the natural border of the Vistula.

'The agricultural holdings in this area are flourishing, the hamlets orderly and with decent buildings; in some of them are manors and smaller comfortable houses, and around most of them there are orchards, canals, apiaries, hop plantations, watermills and windmills,' wrote Wincenty Gawarecki in praise of the area in his *Topographical and Historical Description of the Land of Dobrzyń* a century and a half ago.

One can accept some of his words but one rejects others. The villages are orderly and well built. The signposts bear good Polish names: Fabianki, Światkowizna, Lisek.

After a fifteen-minute drive, a sign saying 'Popowo' appears. It announces a village with a road running through the centre but no square, and smallholdings scattered all over the place. A few buildings huddle round a lane to one side; at the end, the house of the village elder.

His wife assures me: 'Yes, Wałęsa was born here with us.'

I ask her if there are any of his relations in the village. No, none. Wałęsa, as far as she knows, was born during the Occupation. And as always during a war people moved around, leaving their own regions to escape from the Germans. Perhaps his parents at Popowo were hiding somewhere. They themselves wondered, when they heard how famous Wałęsa had become, where he might have been born, in which house. The older people who remembered those times thought that it was in a building which had been demolished. It had been a large house, and three families

lived in it, during the war, all strangers. The older people remember that a baby was born there.

'Wałęsa most certainly comes from here. The priest told us this
at midnight mass. He would not have told us that if he was not
certain.' The village elder's wife supports her statements with the
authority of the priest. He refers me to somebody called
Śmigielski, a native of the village, who now works at Łochocin.
He had worked with Wałęsa, so must know more about him.

'But will he want to talk? Because he's now a party secretary
there,' adds the woman.

I drive back in the direction of Włocławek and see in the
distance an engineering works: a large building with some sheds.
There is a small parking place between the road and the gate
to the works. On one side, a row of glass-fronted showcases.
Inside photographs of foremen, old slogans and one new one:
'Solidarity'.

Śmigielski, a middle-aged man, appears at the porter's lodge
when called on the loudspeaker. He leads me to his office, across
a shed filled with tractors. We enter a tiny office where he has
his desk; he is senior foreman in charge of assessing what repairs
are needed.

He repeats the conjectures of the elder's wife: Wałęsa might have
been born at Popowo, but his parents did not come from here.
How does he know? He has been living at Popowo nearly half
a century, he knows everybody, the family tree of each inhabitant.

He met Wałęsa only here, at the factory.

'He joined after school. We worked in the same workshop, in
the old factory on the other side of the road. We had no
electrician, so he was allotted the job of repairing electric trailers.
He learned it quickly. He was a bright boy, very quick in the
uptake and practical. After two years he was drafted into the army,
and after that he moved to our branch at Lenie. He went there
because he had family in the neighbourhood, somewhere beyond
Chalin, if I remember rightly. Perhaps some of his relations still live
there ...'

From a biography: 'He went to primary school at Chalin.'
A hamlet also on the map, but situated at the other end of the

Włocławek region just on the border of the Płock region. From
Popowo, it is twenty kilometres, by cross-country roads. At Chalin
I learn that Popowo is very near, only three kilometres away. Only
it is another Popowo. And Wałęsa was not born in the first, but
in the second one. The district of Lipno reaches that far and has
two hamlets with the same name. The first one is bigger, on a
main road ...

So I start again on my journey in search of Wałęsa, after being
reassured at the rectory at Sobowo that I am on the right track.
An entry in an old parish register leaves no doubt about where
Wałęsa was born.

From the centre of Chalin, overlooked by an intricate old
windmill, a side road, covered with sand, leads to an open field.
Along the sides of the road are old knobbly willows. On the
horizon, a few scattered buildings, hardly even a hamlet. I stop
in front of a house that seems to be the last one; beyond it lies
only a birch grove and then complete emptiness.

A peasant appears at the door, aroused by the barking of his
dog. He explains how to get to 'the seat of the Wałęsas': cross the
courtyard; beyond the barn there is a path leading to a pond; go
around it, cross the little grove and there will be the house I am
looking for.

'It's empty,' the woman who had also come to the door, warns
me. She invites me to enter the house. I promise to call on my
way back.

I reach the birch grove, where the grass grows high. Beyond
it a meadow and a solitary small hut and an equally small cowshed.
Walls covered with a cement mixture, in each one a small window.
Around it some plum trees. The door is locked.

I return to the house, where I was invited in. The Kosztowny,
the nearest neighbours of the Wałęsa, are well versed in the past
history of local families.

'Do I remember Leszek?' The landlady smiles, repeating my
question. 'Of course, I remember. When we got married, he had
just started school and went to it across our courtyard. He was
well brought up, always said good morning. He was not on speaking
terms with his uncle, but always said good morning to him. A
good child, he had a hard childhood. He had no father, only a
stepfather. His father died just after the war. We were taken in

the last year of the war to Młyniec, near Toruń. To dig trenches and lay fascines by the River Drwęca. Bolek, Lech's father, did not want to dig. They came to fetch him, took him away, beat him up and brought him to Młyniec. We were taken later to Golubie, where we were building a bridge, and Bolek was left behind. At Golubie the barracks were heated, those at Młyniec were not. And this was in winter. Can you imagine: to lie on the bed under a single cover, in the cold. Your hair froze to the wall. Bolek became ill from that beating and the cold. He left four little ones. Lech's mother married the second Wałęsa, Bolek's brother Stanisław, who was unmarried. He was the youngest of the seven Wałęsas. I knew Leszek's father's brothers, for I was born in twenty-six. I was brought up with them. The eldest, Edward, I know only from a photograph because he was killed in the First World War. I also remember the grandparents, and even one great-grandfather. A large farmer, the whole settlement on the hill was his, seventy-five hectares. He came from Kujawy. People said he was a manager of an estate. The paternal grand-father also had a large holding, over twenty hectares. A political man. They said he belonged to the POW (Polish Military Organi-zation), that Piłsudski was hiding at his house for a time. So the older people here say. He would not burn a newspaper before reading everything in it. He did not buy cigarettes, only a pack of tobacco for 38 grosze, tore off a piece of newspaper and made a smoke. He saved the newspaper – he had to read everything in it, read everything that was there ... And the grandfather on his mother's side, Kamiński, was quite a fellow, no fool. Had a lot of spirit. Wore a moustache. Both grandfathers had whiskers. He was well read, used to take the *Pomorzanin*. He knew every-thing, had heard of everything. Kamiński was a local man – his family had lived in the Land of Dobrzyń for generations ...'

'Large families,' says Kosztowna, interrupting her husband. 'Wałęsa's grandfather, how many children would he have had? Something like twenty, with two wives ...

'They were dividing these hectares, and dividing again, until only strips of field remained. So that Lech's father had three hectares, and Stanisław took his part of it. Lech's father lived by carpentry. With his brother, they built barns and cowsheds. They were good craftsmen, the best in the area.

'When Bolek died, there were four children. From the second marriage there were three. So that, if Leszek really is from here, he comes from poverty. First they lived in a clay cottage. Only afterwards did his stepfather build that brick house.

'They went to America, to her mother. The stepfather is still there today. Lech's mother returned, in a coffin. She's buried at the cemetery at Sobowo, next to her first husband.

'A very religious woman. A kind woman, with a heart of gold.

'The boys grew up into decent men. Edward is a civil engineer in Kutno. Stanisław lives in Bydgoszcz. Well, and Leszek ...

'Every school holidays, he would go to the brick works. A slight child – he carried and stacked bricks to earn a few złotys. But he made his way in life ...

'For so many years we had not heard a word from him, and then suddenly – on television.'

They said they knew of the strike at Gdańsk, but not much about it. There was the harvest, work in the fields. Their hamlet is off the beaten track – the papers don't get there. And suddenly they heard on television that Wałęsa was leading this great strike.

'Should one believe it or not?' Kosztowny wonders to this day.

At the primary school at Chalin there are no longer any of the teachers who taught Wałęsa. The school is in an old mansion house of the last century, a wooden structure with a porch propped up by two slight columns. Inside, a squeaking staircase and floors with rotten wooden tiles. For years there had been no money for repairs.

'Perhaps now we shall get some? They say that Solidarity has got a larger allocation for education in the budget,' the teachers say hopefully.

They don't know Wałęsa, but know everything about him.

'He's famous in the world, so with us as well. Television is everywhere.'

Out of curiosity they looked into all the daybooks. He was an average pupil; not in any way outstanding.

Mrs Lewandowska, who lives in a beautiful villa in the very centre of the village, was in the same class as Lech. She has a photograph of the fifth form during an outing. She keeps it on top of the sideboard, together with Wałęsa's photograph cut out from a newspaper, taken during his visit to Rome.

'Here he is, and there am I. And here he is with the Pope,' she explains, attracting a little glory to herself.

Did he do particularly well at school? She cannot remember, so many years have passed, almost thirty, although ...

'We sometimes went to the lake after school. He liked to show off his courage – he always swam furthest. Well, he has gone far in his life as well, very far.'

From the biography: 'He completed his studies at the Secondary Trade School in Lipno.'

Lipno is a smallish town of fifteen thousand inhabitants. It is surrounded on three sides by the River Mień; to the north there is a high hill. One of those small towns with a long and interesting history, with periods of splendour. In the past it had been an important administrative centre, the place of assembly for the Land of Dobrzyń nobility. Today it has lost its importance and life there goes on without undue haste. In guidebooks it mentions that Pola Negri, the famous silent cinema star, the most beautiful woman in the world, was born there. Her real name was Apolonia Chałupiec; by her first marriage she was Countess Dombska, by her second one Princess Mdivani.

'I understand that Wałęsa is a pretext.' The Mayor of Lipno, Janusz Wikaryjczyk, tried to guess my intentions. 'A pretext to be interesting about our town. Taking Pola Negri as the point of departure.'

The city council is located in the town hall, on the roof of which is a four-cornered turret with a small figure of an angel crowning it.

'This was made by Pola's dad. He was a roofer,' the Mayor assures me. And tells me how before the war the social committee for the building of a grammar school applied to their famous fellow countrywoman for a donation. She sent some dollars, but it was not a remarkable sum. At Lipno they are sure that she is still alive, although she was born in 1896.

'There were proposals, even recently, to invite her here. A woman with dollars, perhaps she would leave something to the town ...'

Another notable person was born at Lipno, the great actor Wincenty Rapacki, who played in the Kraków and Warsaw theatres and left some plays. Since we are speaking about famous people, here is a suitable quotation:

'The local citizens are the descendants and heirs of men famous for their loyalty to the Motherland and for their readiness to make sacrifices. The just verdict of history should properly appreciate those worthy citizens, the dwellers in the Land of Dobrzyń, who during our lifetime have glorified the Polish land by their splendid deeds.'

Lipno had many local patriots who don't allow the history of their land to sink into the darkness of oblivion. Recently the lovers of the Land of Dobrzyń were presented with the keys to a museum.

'A museum sounds perhaps too pompous,' the Mayor says. 'It will be rather a remembrance room. A few documents and exhibits we wish to show. There will be a corner devoted to Pola Negri and Wincenty Rapacki, perhaps in the future also to Wałęsa'.

'If he wins,' adds the Mayor's secretary, Ptaszyński.

'And proves to be a very strong man. There is a basis for it: in the chronicles of the local school it is noted that he was its pupil. For the moment, people are interested not in his person, but in his ideas. In the Trade School, a branch of Solidarity had already been formed by November 1980. How could we not support our ex-pupil?'

Ptaszyński is also interested in Wałęsa's personality, because he has many characteristics of a typical Land of Dobrzyń man. He mentions openness, courage, perseverance, receptiveness to change, and adds that these are characteristics of the people of the borderlands, which is what the Land of Dobrzyń had been for centuries.

Ptaszyński is fascinated by history. He travels through the centuries with great ease. He reminds me that Długosz, the chronicler, wrote about the Castle of Dobrzyń, for many years a frontier castle of the Mazovian princes and attacked by Prussians and Lithuanians, later by Knights of the Cross. During the Nobles' Republic the area between the Vistula, the Drwęcą and the Skrwą was a separate unit with its own *seymik* (minor Sejm). It was inhabited by petty nobility, without serfs, but very ambitious. After the Partitions, the Land of Dobrzyń found itself on the periphery of the Kingdom of Poland, then of the Principality of Warsaw and of Congress Poland.* On the border of the partitioners. And lastly on the periphery of the province of Warsaw after the First War, and of the province of Pomerania after the Second.

'I was formerly employed by the district council. The district of Lipno spreads beyond Dobrzyń. I travelled a lot through the villages. Many farmers, especially in the regions adjoining the one from which Wałęsa comes, have their family crests. They are poor, but not without ambition. Very good farmers, skilled in agriculture. They were never any trouble, were interested in social problems and determined to achieve their rightful aims. The rural self-government functioned well here even in unfavourable conditions. If they are convinced that something is to their advantage they will never give in. You could talk to them during meetings for ten hours at a time, and in the end they would even agree with you. But, on leaving, when already in the doorway, they would say: "And yet it's we who are right." Wałęsa is rather like that.

'A good man of Dobrzyń,' the Mayor sums up, and explains to me how to reach the Trade School where many teachers remember him. The school is outside the town, under a high hill, St Anthony's Mount. The director, Jerzy Rybacki, has at hand a large thick book. He is prepared to give information about his famous pupil.

'Here it is, in 1958: number 1,488. Lech Wałęsa, the son of Bolesław and Feliksa. Father's trade: smallholder.' In the school year 1958/9 he attended Class I B – he reads the entry in the register. 'That was the class for agricultural mechanization.'

'At first we wondered whether this was our pupil or not. The data fitted, his appearance as well. We dug out the notes to see how he did at school. He was average. In the final report he has two "fours": in the economics of rural enterprises and in physical training. And one "five": in behaviour. He was worst in history. In one of the forms he had "twos" during three school periods. A man who is now creating history.'

* The Third Partition (1795) divided what remained of Poland between Russia, Prussia and Austria. Napoleon revived the short-lived 'Grand Duchy of Warsaw' (1807–13), which was granted some degree of independence. But after his defeat, the Congress of Vienna restored the Partition. The Russian share of Poland after 1815 was known as the 'Congress Kingdom'.

In another book, reports from the hostel where he stayed. The first one: He smokes and beats others up. The second: Lech Wałęsa walks about with his head bare, although his cap is in his pocket. And the third: '17.4.1961: I suggest that Lech Wałęsa should be given only a "four" for behaviour.'

'He was three times called before the teachers' council to be punished for smoking cigarettes in the hostel.'

Gryczewski, a teacher who works in the school's workshops, gives a character sketch of his former pupil: a bit of a bully, but ·a likeable one. A happy disposition can disarm even the most angry teachers.

Director Rybacki was at the time starting his work in the hostel, as its head.

'I remember Leszek, although I have forgotten many of the others. Why? He was an extremely well-organized boy. If one suggested to him that he should try to lead a group, he would be irreplaceable. To give you an example: The hostel inmates had to sweep out the corridors. Each hall took it in turns for a week at a time. When the turn of Wałęsa's hall came the teacher didn't have to worry or urge them on. At half past six in the morning, he would wake them up, pick the boys who would wash the floor and those who would polish it. By the time the teacher got up, the floor shone. I was reminiscing with some colleagues recently and we all agreed: there was already something in him at that time, some definite organizing talent.'

He looks again at the register.

'He finished school in 1961. He worked at the State Machinery Centre (POM), and later, as is the case with many of our graduates, the love for the sea prevailed and he went to the shipyards. Many of our pupils work there.'

From the biography: 'He came to Gdańsk in 1967 and began work in the shipyards as an electrician.'

I visit the personnel and 'work humanization' department. It occupies several rooms in a building situated near No. 2 Gate. On the ground floor the Works Commission of Solidarity is located. From the windows one can see the monument, the one erected after August, to honour the dead shipyard workers.

I am turning the pages of a grey folder, 61878, Lech Wałęsa's works number. Between stiff covers lies a short history of his nine-year period of work, noted on several forms, loose pages and slips of paper.

He applied for work on 30 May 1967 with a letter from the Employment Office: 'I am applying for ...' On the reverse side personal details. Under the rubric 'military service' the entry: Corporal of the Reserves. Marital status: Unmarried. Membership of social organizations: ZMW (Union of Rural Youth).

Admission document: On 2 June 1967 Wałęsa began work as a ship's electrician in section W-4.

He was allotted to a brigade led by the skilled worker Alois Mosiński, one of the shipyard's veterans. Since November 1980, Mosiński has been a pensioner. I visit him at his home. He lives in a suburb of Sopot, in a quiet side street. We are talking in his garden: I have caught him watering his flowerbeds.

'Wałęsa came from a State Machinery Centre; he said he earned too little there. Somebody must have directed him to us – perhaps recruiters, who brought people from all over Poland. He was not familiar with the job on a ship, so at first I had to watch him a little. He was young, saw a ship for the first time, was interested in everything. He was bright and eager. Disciplined, never late for work. What else? He liked being in a brigade and fitted in well. He was talkative, curious about people and things. I had twenty people in my brigade, electricians and fitters. He was allotted to work in the first ten.'

Henryk Lenarciak, a fitter, also belonged to Mosiński's brigade. Ten years older than Wałęsa, he began work in the shipyard in 1952. In December 1970 he was on the strike committee. After August, he was elected president of the social committee for building the monument to fallen shipyard workers in 1970.

'I worked on the same ship as Wałęsa. I cannot tell you much about the first period. He was a rather quiet boy. Didn't stand out. Sometimes he would speak at meetings, but not too roughly. I heard that in March 1968 he advised the workers not to go to a mass meeting at which the students were to be publicly censored. He came to the front in December 1970. Events of those days carried him upwards. It was then that his talent for leadership was first shown.'

From the biography: 'In 1970 he actively participated in the strike which broke out in the shipyard after the rise in prices.'

The price rises were published on the evening of Saturday, 12 December. On the following Monday, in front of the building of the Directorate of the Gdańsk shipyard, a crowd gathered. The first to stop work were workers from the 'Esses' – from departments S-3 and S-4.

Lenarciak: 'In the morning I went to the ship. When I returned to the department for breakfast, the common room was full of people. They were sitting on the tables, discussing something. The break finished but no one was eager to return to work. An electro-mechanic rushed in and said that the Esses were idle. Immediately afterwards the news: the Esses are in front of the Directorate. We went there too ...'

The workers were coming from all sides, in overalls and helmets. Several thousand people gathered in the square in front of the directorate. They demanded the withdrawal of the price rises and talks with the authorities. No one came. The crowd left the shipyard and went to the building of the Regional Committee of the Polish United Workers Party (KW PZPR). Later the procession, many thousands strong, marched through the Gdańsk shipyard as far as the North Yard, summoning people to join the strike. The Gdańsk Polytechnic and the building of the Polish Radio were the next ports of call. On the return trip from Wrzeszcz, on the Błędnik bridge, there occurred the first clash with the militia, who tried to bar their way.

Lenarciak: 'As far as I know Wałęsa didn't leave the ship for his breakfast that day, so he didn't take part in the demonstration in front of the directorate and he was not amongst those who left the shipyard. He left the ship only at the end of his shift. But on the Tuesday, he found himself at the head of the march.'

Early that morning a procession formed in the shipyard and marched on the city. This time it was not to the Regional Committee building, but to the city police headquarters in Swierczewski Street. About 8 am part of the ground floor of that building was occupied. That was probably when the first shots were heard and the first victims were killed. The authorities brought tanks into action. The only possibility of defending the occupied positions was to attack the forces of the militia by driving vehicles at them at high speed. An escalation of tension followed; the workforce decided to burn the Regional Committee building. By about 10 am it was on fire. In the region of the Main Station down to Hucisko a regular battle was raging. There were over 20,000 workers ... this description of the events of that Tuesday is based We went to the directorate building, where in the large hall on Solidarity.

And Wałęsa? From reports that I studied it appears that he was on the march, at its head. Somebody said that he spoke from the top of a telephone booth. When the ground floor of the police headquarters was occupied, he unexpectedly appeared at a first-floor window. He appealed for the planned attack on the nearby gaol to be called off. And the crowd obeyed him, and withdrew.

After the return to the shipyard, a sit-in strike was declared.

Lenarciak: 'We met in the department to elect delegates for the strike committee. In our section Wałęsa and myself were elected. We went to the Directorate building, where in the large hall on the first floor several people were waiting. The committee dealt mainly with order in the shipyard, with security on the ships. Every man watched over his sector. We organized work shifts and food supplies. I was liaising between the department and the committee, and Wałęsa was one of those who were directing the strike action.'

The historian Alexander Klemp, who, in the Local Trade Committee of Solidarity in Gdańsk, was entrusted with the job of establishing the true course of the December events, says: 'Our investigations reveal that Wałęsa was one of the most active men in the strike committee. At the start, it consisted of many people, but later it comprised only five, a kind of praesidium. There was no chairman, probably for reasons of security.'

In the second half of January, after a period of calm, tension rose again. The price rises were not cancelled, and changes took place slowly. On 16 January a list of demands was published. Among these: 'Trade unions at all levels should consist of non-party members.' The last demand was: 'We demand that Edward Gierek should come and talk to the workers and not to the activists.' On 24 January the shipyard went on strike.

Lenarciak: 'The next morning it was announced that the work-force was to elect three delegates. It was said that the delegates from the shipyard were to go to Warsaw, to meet the authorities.

They elected Wałęsa, Suszek and myself. We got parcels with food, and buses were provided. After several hours of waiting, we were brought to the building of the Regional National Council at Gdańsk.

Thus Wałęsa participated in the meeting with Gierek and Jaroszewicz. He did not speak. It was agreed that Lenarciak was to speak for their section.

A month later trade-union elections for the section councils were held at last, fully democratic, as the people demanded. Lenarciak was elected chairman; Wałęsa was elected to fulfil the function of section work inspector.

'He wanted a job that would allow him to wander around the shipyard and to visit all the ships. He said that he wanted to keep his finger on the pulse of the shipyard, to know what was happening. The job he got gave him these facilities.'

At the end of February, Jan Tetter, a reporter on the *Głos Wybrzeza* (*Voice of the Coast*), had conversations with a few men who at that period obtained some authority amongst the workforce and became their authentic representatives.

'By chance, the three people named were elected officers of the trade unions in their sectors. They were elected freely, without anybody's support or suggestion, genuinely on behalf of the crew. This proves a refreshing fact – that people keen for action have opportunities in the life of their workplace. They are faced with a hard task, representing the interests of the crew. Will they be able to fulfil the functions they have undertaken? Will they be worthy of the confidence they have gained and fulfil the hopes of the crew? Only time will tell. Yet their energy and their obvious good intentions awake general sympathy.'

Among the three workers featured by the *Voice of the Coast* was also Lech Wałęsa, electrician:

'It is said that experience comes with age. Of course, but it also comes with action. Only analysis and minute examination of one's actions lead to reflection. The electrician on section W-4, freshly appointed with Henryk Lenarciak, member of the section trade organization, was a controversial figure. He was twenty-seven years old, had read books about the psychology of crowds, about spontaneous action. The previous months had not spared him involvement in both unexpected and dangerous actions. It so happened that he was at the centre of the events which everybody was discussing. It was not for fun, not from a thirst for adventure or hatred of people responsible for law and order; he simply assessed his situation as one in which there was nothing to lose, so he got involved very deeply in the leadership of the shipyard strike. Politicians live more intensive lives. The experiences of this young man can be compared with those of men in their middle years. He looks at himself from the perspective of some years later, soberly, and realizes that today he would have acted differently and would have been more realistic in considering what is possible and what is dangerous. Has he changed? Quite possibly. Lech Wałęsa has been working in the shipyard for four years. He lives with his wife and child in a rented room, for which he pays 800 złoty a month, of which the shipyard pays half. He is popular among the workers in his section.

'Popularity is a tricky thing. I consider that at present one must not talk, but act and work. Talk will not achieve anything. I consider that the section council should always be in touch with people and account for the people's trust, but act in a way which does not disorganize production. Even in this area things are improving, just as in human relationships. If people trust us, we in the trade-union organization will also do our bit. We all wish for things to improve.'

'Active and stubborn', Lenarciak says about Wałęsa's activities on the council. 'He was trying to impose his own opinion. Sometimes, when we thought differently, he would say that he would go to the workforce and tell them what his proposals were and the workforce would support him without fail.'

After a year new elections to the section council were held because they were due by law; the previous election was held before the appointed time. The composition of the council was not much changed. The only one who withdrew his candidature was Wałęsa.

Lenarciak, who was elected chairman for the second time, considers that disappointment was the reason for Wałęsa's resignation. Not with the activities in the section, because there much had been changed for the better, but with things on a higher level, which continued as before and where one could not overcome bureaucratic routine. Unimportant matters were being decided at section level; more important ones were decided without asking the workers their opinion. Wałęsa did not like this, as he saw the role and position of the unions differently.

In his personal documentation, that whole period of his life is covered by two scraps of paper. 'Reported change in the worker's circumstances' is the first one; 'married on 8 November 1969'. The second, in 1972, records a change of address, to Gdańsk-Stogi, 26C Wrzosowa Street, apartment 5.

The small estate of four-storey apartment blocks stands apart, quite a way from the end of the tram line which goes as far as the most beautiful beach at Gdańsk. The estate borders on a little coastal wood and a group of allotments.

The Parol family were for many years the nearest neighbours of the Wałęsas. They lived at No. 4. Henryk Parol was also a shipyard worker on section M-Y. He says that he met Wałęsa back in 1964, in the army. They served together at Koszalin in an artillery unit. Wałęsa had already done one year's service at the time.

'He was then a section leader for new recruits, a corporal. He liked discipline, was exacting but understanding. He didn't harass anybody for the hell of it. He achieved more by a joke and a sense of humour than others did by shouting. His best joke was when he came into the cookhouse and asked "What's rustling here?" and we would shout back: "Wałęsa's whiskers."'

Parol met him again after many years in a shipyard hostel.

'I was walking down a passage, and there was Wałęsa. He didn't recognize me. "What's rustling?" I asked. He stopped. I reminded him that we had served in the army together. I told him the names of my colleagues and reminded him of various jokes. Then he believed me. He seemed mistrustful. I didn't know that he had led the strike in December and had had trouble afterwards. This was in 1971. A year later I was allotted a flat and it transpired that Wałęsa was my neighbour.'

Lenarciak remembers that in 1973 Wałęsa was nearly sacked from the shipyard. At that time the first 'December strikers' began to be dismissed. The pretexts varied. The skilled worker Nowicki, for instance, was sacked because he participated in the strike committee and later was elected chairman of the council on S-5. He was black-listed and could not get work anywhere. Wałęsa was threatened with the sack because he made a comment on the authorities, something derogatory. Somebody informed the secretary of the Party organization and he referred it higher up. The section council intervened and vetoed the sacking. There were no reservations about his work – Mosiński's brigade was considered one of the best in the shipyard. It had a good reputation. There was never any trouble about work deliveries, and the shipowners were pleased.

'We saved him from dismissal, but he had to promise to keep his mouth shut.'

In 1976, from section W-4 a letter was sent to the directorate and the works council 'informing them about the intention of cancelling the work contract with Citizen Lech Wałęsa by immediate notice'. The grounds were: 'Employee difficult in collaboration. Tendentious and malicious public statements about the sections' managerial staff and political and social organizations which create a bad working climate in the section.' The letter was signed by the manager of the section.

What had brought this about?

On 11 February an extraordinary meeting was held in the section. It was the end of the section council's four-year term. Wałęsa spoke at the meeting. The skilled worker Mosiński remembers that he was applauded. The ship's crew had supported him.

Lenarciak, who was at the end of his term on the council, remembers even more. Before the meeting he spoke to Wałęsa, who warned him that he would speak sharply. 'You are too soft in your dealings, one must be more decisive!' he said.

'He spoke for quite a long time. One sentence I still remember: it was that Gierek had misled the nation, didn't keep any of his promises, that he acted without asking the working class for their opinion. That was the sentence which was most applauded and which caused Wałęsa's dismissal. A representative of the directorate came to the meeting, someone from the top ranks of production. He was indignant: how dare Wałęsa criticize a man of such splendid character? He was cross with the secretary of the Party organization and the manager of the section because they had not interrupted. A few days later I learned from the chairman of the section council, my successor, that Wałęsa intended to give up his job. My successor asked me what he should do? I said: "Everything to save him: there is no criticism of his work and for criticism at a meeting one cannot sack anybody." The manager of the section was then Mr Konkel, a civil engineer. He had received an instruction to dismiss Wałęsa. He did not sign the document, and stopped being manager. We were told that he had resigned because of ill-health, but later a representative of the directorate told us otherwise. He said that if the instructions were not obeyed, not only the manager would be sacked. The new manager signed Wałęsa's dismissal document a day after taking on his position. He was not a bad fellow, but cowardly. He's dead now. He was found in the vicinity of the House of Technicians in Gdańsk ... In 1979 ...'

The section council did not sign the dismissal notice. It was authorized by the chairman of the works council, Mieczysław Umiński, and countersigned 'by instruction of the directorate' by the then manager of the personnel department, Stefan Borkowski. From the date of this notice, Wałęsa was forbidden entry to the shipyard.

'In the period of notice we won't require the services of the citizen in the shipyard, but for the period from 19.3.76 to 30.4.76, the shipyard will pay Citizen Wałęsa his wages as for the holiday period.'

In his references they wrote: 'He finished the master course of the Society of Polish Electrical Engineers. His work was good. He was not decorated, there were no distinctions. He worked socially as section work inspector, performing these functions well. He was a good colleague. There is no criticism of his work discipline. No penal proceedings are instigated. The contract was dissolved according to the rules.'

Wałęsa took recourse to the law and appealed to the District Labour Appeal Commission. The commission did not find any formal irregularities, but it had the duty to investigate whether a dismissal was justified. The committee of judges, presided over by a woman, Judge Szkolnicka, decided that criticism at a union meeting is sufficient ground to dismiss an employee from work.

Lenarciak: 'During that meeting they elected Wałęsa as delegate to the works' Union Conference. They were afraid that he would speak there, that he would be elected to the Regional Conference and perhaps even higher. Therefore they dismissed him as a delegate and did not have to worry any more!'

From the biography: 'In 1976, he began work as an electrician in the ZREMB enterprise.'

The four-storey building adjoins a road; there is a vast hall, covered with a kind of cupola. The establishment spreads out over the land between the railway and the road to Tczew. There is a riverhead not far away. Two large notices say what is produced there: 'machinery and implements for cement mixing' and 'machines and implements for earth moving'.

In the front building on the second floor a small room belongs to Solidarity. Its chairman, Zygmunt Woynicz, has Wałęsa's folder on his desk. Recently a commission at the factory analysed whether the dismissal of Wałęsa could be considered as an act of reprisal. Technically it cannot. In that factory, unlike the shipyards, they got rid of him in a more sophisticated manner, preserving all appearances.

They hired him for the transport section on 3 May 1976, a section which is located in a different place, away from the directorate, on the banks of the Dead Vistula.

'He was a good craftsman; quick,' I hear from people who worked with him there. 'He was a motor-car electrician; he could not bear a faulty car. He fiddled with it until he made it work. He was never drunk, never late. In a workshop situated away from the main offices, this is not often the case. The boss was pleased with him. So, when they insisted that he should give a bad testimonial to Wałęsa, he refused. And they insisted, because Wałęsa began his activities with the free trade unions.'

The Founding Committee of these unions was established in Gdańsk on the eve of 1 May 1978. The initiator was electrical engineer Andrzej Gwiazda. Wałęsa had known him before, so when the committee was formed he became one of its most active members. He also joined the editorial offices of the *Coastal Worker*.

'The basis of our activities was meetings and discussions,' writes Joanna Duda-Gwiazda, an activist of free trade unions. 'We met in small groups, always changing the meeting place, sometimes meeting in forests. The security police infiltrated larger meetings or those held too often in one place. There were lectures on work law, on modern history etc. At other meetings we referred to our attempts to change our system of government during the last thirty-five years. The need for the self-organization of society was the logical outcome of those lectures. Most meetings were devoted to the current problems of works, factories and the country as a whole ... We were discussing, too, the structure of trade unions within our system ...'

In the first number of *Coastal Worker*, which was published in August 1978, the following declaration appeared: 'We do not have political aims, we do not wish to impose on our members, collaborators and sympathizers any precise political or social views, we do not aim to take over power. We realize, however, that we will not be free from accusations that we are indulging in political activities. The range of matters considered in our country to be political is very wide and encompasses almost everything except excursions to collect mushrooms.'

'Wałęsa brought leaflets and proclamations,' remembers Franciszek Bogdański, an employee of the workshops in Siennicka Street. 'They were snatched up in a minute. I frequently had to go to the Jelcz factory for chassis. Wałęsa gave me leaflets and, during the journey, I threw them into the streets of larger towns. I also distributed them in factories. They were read with interest and people asked for more. I helped Wałęsa to stick up posters on walls before the December festivals. In the directorate building I once replaced a leaflet which one of the employees had previously torn down. Later he was repairing part of an engine and it fell on his leg and broke it. Lech told him then: "Remember: somebody stuck up truth on the wall; don't touch it again; God has punished you." Wałęsa was observed very closely. Once we went to a funeral together. When it was over, I said: "Come to my place, we'll have a coffee ..." "I'd rather not, not now," he answered. "I'm being watched. If I call on you they might later search your flat." They were watching him. I was an undercover activist, yet I was being called by the police and advised not to have anything to do with Wałęsa. To him they suggested that he should leave the free unions, that if he did they would help him in his career.'

In November 1978 the management of ZREMB addressed a notice to the works council that it intended 'to cancel with notice as from 31 December 1978 the work agreement with Citizen Lech Wałęsa, employee in the Transport Section'.

They gave as grounds for it that he was redundant:

'The programme of production for the year 1979 requires the increase in the workforce in direct production by about fifty people without a planned increase in the workforce as a whole. The allocation of this number of jobs can only be made by reducing employment in indirect production and in the group of white-collar workers. Citizen Lech Wałęsa has qualifications as an electrical engineer in direct production. With these qualifications, because of the full complement of electrical engineers in direct production with a longer term of employment, it is not possible to transfer Citizen Wałęsa. Moreover we beg to inform the works council that, in conformity with the decision of the assistant director of technical workshops, the post of electrical engineer in the Transport Section will be abolished.'

The manager of the personnel section stated that the dismissal was justified. The choice of Wałęsa had been made by pressure from outside. At that time people were very interested in him. Who? Several times the works were visited by an officer from the regional police headquarters who looked at Wałęsa's personal file. He later talked with the director. There must have been a connection between this visit and his future dismissal.

The good opinion given by the manager of the section did not help. 'He is very independent, has high professional qualifications (within the wide area of his speciality). He is an employee who shows considerable initiative in solving difficulties and technical and organizational problems, especially when faced with difficult and complicated tasks outside his own scope of work. He is a disciplined worker, conscientious and friendly. He has a great ability for creating a collective atmosphere of friendly co-operation with colleagues.'

Franciszek Bogdański: 'The manager told the truth. His opinion was badly received. He did not change it and stopped being manager. He was transferred to the stores, and lost two thousand złotys a month in wages.'

The motion of the management was presented for the works council's approval. It agreed to Wałęsa's dismissal.

Edward Chrust was the chairman of the council at the time:

'Today we can tell the truth. There were pressures from the management to dismiss him. They gave two reasons: "moonlighting" and redundancies. Well, Wałęsa owned an old "Warszawa" car and sometimes repaired it in the works. After hours, in his own time, but they claimed that the management had not been informed. The manager of the workshop knew, but they said this wasn't enough. Had it been only the question of those repairs, our council would not have consented to his dismissal. Other employees also made repairs. But we were informed that the post of electrician in the Transport Section would be liquidated. Towards the end of the year they always looked for redundancies in auxiliary and administrative production, though not so much in the latter. Now we know that they were looking for a pretext to sack Wałęsa. Why should it have been he and not another employee? His work was good, he was often praised. There were no accusations other than his work in the free unions. He did not conceal it. What had turned the scales? There was an instruction that workers elected by the brigade should join the Conference of Workers' Self-Government.* They were to make up one third of the complement. Wałęsa was elected by the Transport Section. And at the first meeting of the Conference he spoke, critically. He asked how the proposed programme of the self-government activities was designed, why was it brought ready-made in an attaché-case? Then the campaign was launched. They had to find something incriminating. And they found that alleged private work in working hours and the redundancy. We, as a body, could not oppose the redundancy, because it was legally instituted. Only when Wałęsa appealed and presented his private situation – he was the only breadwinner in a family of six – could we apply to the directorate to keep him on at the works. We suggested his transfer to the Senior Mechanic's section.

'At the meeting of the District Appeal Committee, the directorate consented to withdraw the notice and agreed to the works council's suggestion. A compromise was reached.'

Rogacki: 'I asked Wałęsa to accept the document on the change of working conditions. He refused to accept it, saying that work in the section under the Senior Mechanic didn't suit him, that he wouldn't be an errand boy.'

* The Conferences of Workers' Self-Government, set up in 1958, were factory parliaments designed to neutralize the spontaneous workers' councils which had arisen in the revolutionary atmosphere of 1956. Composed of workers' council delegates, trade-union officials and members of the factory Communist Party branch, the Conferences in practice restored Party authority over the labour force.

The refusal was considered a grievous infringement of an employee's duties, and on 29 December he was again given notice. Bogdański: 'When we learned that he was sacked, we were furious. We decided to protest. I spoke about it with Wałęsa. He dissuaded me from my intention to organize a strike. "Don't struggle," he said. "You and the others will be sacked. You've got children, don't expose yourself. We're not strong enough yet. The time will come that we shall be stronger than they, then we shall act. Not everything is ready as yet." I cried when he went.'

From the biography: 'In May 1979 he was taken on for work in the "Electromontage" enterprise.'

The workshop is located just outside the Gdańsk district of Stogi, between the railway line leading to the North Harbour and the road turning into Westerplatte. Here electrical equipment is produced, there are stores and a motor vehicle shed.

Florian Wiśniewski, a senior skilled worker, a long-term employee of Electromontage and during the August strike a member of the praesidium of the works council, relates:

'Wałęsa quickly gained the reputation of the best automobile electrician, bar none. From the moment of his arrival at Electromontage, he was under observation. On the pavement in front of the works an unfamiliar car was parked, plain-clothes men were wandering about and from time to time they called at the works. Wałęsa sometimes went to building sites to repair equipment. Immediately afterwards functionaries of the security forces would appear on the site and ask what he had been doing, who were his contacts, what did he talk about? In spite of this, he gained more and more sympathizers for the idea of free unions, both in the works and on building sites. He brought literature, began discussions. He had an incredible facility for establishing contacts and what he said about the role of the free trade unions seemed to convince his listeners. Several people joined the organizing committee. The anniversary of the December events was approaching. Now a car was parked in front of the works permanently. Three days before the anniversary, a second car appeared with a police registration number. There were fears that Wałęsa would be arrested. We considered that everything should be done to enable him to take part in the ceremony of laying wreaths at No. 2 Gate of the shipyard, at the place where his colleagues were shot. He was a strike leader in December, and could not imagine that he would not be involved in the ceremony at such a moment. We arranged that, should the police enter the works compound, Wałęsa would be smuggled out in a container. Everything was prepared. We kept strict control over people entering the works, kept a watch on the area in front of them. Some functionaries came in on the eve of the ceremony. They went first to the offices. At that moment Wałęsa left, not in a container, but in a "Nysa" car. A lot of people knew that it was intended that he would leave in a container, and there were fears that the information might have leaked out. The next day he didn't come to work. He was in hiding.'

The ceremony in front of the gate of the shipyard – according to reports from the participants – was attended by around seven thousand people. The speakers were Maria Płońska of the Young Poland Movement,* the instigators of the idea of holding a ceremony of the anniversary of the 1970 events, and Lech Wałęsa. He spoke about his experiences of December 1970. At the end he called on all those present to take part in the New Year in building a monument to the victims. If this did not succeed, each participant was to bring a large stone the following year, and a mound would be made of them.

Florian Wiśniewski: 'Soon afterwards redundancies began in our works. Fourteen people were selected for the sack, the majority of them members of the free unions. Only two people out of the fourteen were unconnected with them. The works council was informed. We got together just before Christmas. We knocked the bottom out of the principle of redundancies. At a building site at Kwidzyn for instance there were young pioneers working who had been borrowed from another enterprise. We were short of manpower. The chairman of the council was a man totally under the thumb of the management, but the majority did not agree with the dismissals. The enterprise appealed to the chief management of the Trade Union of Building Workers. First they praised us for defending the employees, and later, when they realized who

* The Young Poland Movement was an opposition group established in 1979. Although its approach was more nationalist and religious than that of the free trade union group to which Wałęsa belonged, the Gdańsk branch of Young Poland was closely involved in the strike movement of August 1980.

were the men to be made redundant, they rejected our protest with regard to a few people, among them Wałęsa. At the same time the management, in order to strengthen their decision by an additional argument, gave Wałęsa a reprimand for absence from work. He was absent on the day when he was in hiding, the day of the anniversary of December last. He appealed to us. At the meeting at which we were to consider his appeal, the director and first secretary of the Works Committee of the Party were present. They must have thought that their presence would exert pressure on the members of the council. We decided that, as someone had agreed to let the police enter the works area, Wałęsa had been forced into hiding. A vote was taken, the majority voting for quashing the reprimand. But they did not revoke the dismissal. At the time a workers' commission for the defence of those who had received notice was created in the workshop. During the breakfast break a meeting was called in the cutting shop. Wałęsa spoke through a loudspeaker. The meeting selected a delegation – a group of fitters – and they went to the management to plead for those dismissed. It was an initiative of the workshop employees themselves. The break in work lasted for a few hours, so one could call this a strike. The management did not give way, Wałęsa and the others had to leave. On every pay-day thereafter we made a collection and in this way we helped those who were dismissed.'

From the biography: 'Until the start of the strike in August 1980, Wałęsa was out of work.'

'Often at that time they were trying to get him,' says Mrs Parol, the neighbour of the Wałęsas. 'The biggest round-up was before Szczepański's funeral. Szczepański had worked with Wałęsa at the Electromontage; they were dismissed at the same time. Szczepański, a young boy who lived not far from here, suddenly disappeared without trace. Later they found his body in a canal. His feet had apparently been cut off and his fingernails pulled out. Many people from Stogi planned to go to the funeral. At night, police lorries came to our estate. At first we thought that it was a raid against the amber-collectors who were digging the forests on the coast, causing terrible damage to the trees. Meanwhile the police surrounded our house. When I looked out of the window in the morning cars stood in front of it, and outside on the staircase were two plain-clothes men. I guessed that they were waiting for Wałęsa. I went and told Wałęsa not to try to leave his flat. He was getting ready to go out. There was a wreath prepared in the passage. I told him the police were round the corner. He answered that he had to go to the funeral, come what may. When he was leaving the block, the plain-clothes men rushed him and tried to grab the wreath, but they didn't get it. Then the next lot rushed out and there was a scuffle. At last they tore the wreath out of his hands and took him to the car. Many people on the estate saw the scene. And it is from that moment that he became known. People began to realize that he was active in some organization.'

'Everything was quiet at the Wałęsas',' adds Mr Parol. 'It was rare for someone to call. Sometimes he would drop in on us, sometimes I would go to him, sometimes we shared a glass. He was not keen to tell me where he was active, and I was not particularly interested either. What did I observe? That he was reading a book called *Psychology of Man*.

'He often used to get taken off to clink. Once they caught him in town. He was walking with one of his children, with little Magda, sticking up some posters. They bundled him into the car together with the pram, drove to his house and left the pram, and then took him away.

'He used to drive a very old wreck of a car on the windows of which he had a copy of the Constitution of the Third of May. They took away his driving licence.'

'This was before the election,' says Edmund Tissler, who lives in the neighbouring block. 'I looked out of the window one morning to see somebody going from staircase to staircase sticking up posters that said: "If you want to starve, vote!" That was Wałęsa. I knew him by sight. From our kitchen I can see their windows. On every church festival they put pictures in the windows. The people wondered who could be living there; perhaps Jehovah's Witnesses. Certainly a very religious family. I often saw him leading his cluster of children to church. There is no more religious family in the whole district.'

'A lot of children, a small flat, they lived modestly. He told me often that if somebody has many children, he understands others who have, and how difficult it is for such large families to make ends meet,' says Parol.

'The sixth child was born when Wałęsa was under arrest. They came for him on the evening that Mrs Wałęsa was about to give birth. She screamed terribly then. "Don't take my husband," she screamed so that the whole block could hear. They let him out in the morning. Afterwards he went into hiding for some time. He was not at home just before the strike in August.'

Henryk Lenarciak met him a few times on the platform of the electric railway by the shipyard. He was distributing leaflets. They also met in the little house in Poznańska Street, owned by Szołoch, who in December was one of the five men directing the strike. The supporters of the free unions met there.

'Wałęsa called on me at home on Sunday, 10 August. He was in a great hurry. He told me that Miss Walentynowicz had been freed, that in a few days there would be a strike in the shipyard. "And I myself will emerge at the right moment," he warned. And so it was.'

From the biography: 'In August 1980 he led the strike at the Gdańsk shipyard.'

In the strike bulletin *Solidarity*, No. 11, one can read about the beginning of the August events:

'Our group is now a vast crowd. We walk up to No. 2 Gate and stop there for a minute. We stand in silence, to honour those who perished in December 1970. We sing the Dabrowski Mazurka (the Polish National Anthem). Now we feel different from how we felt at the beginning. We are aware of our strength. Now we are walking towards the mechanical digger. We transform it into a makeshift rostrum. The crowd surrounds us on all sides ... Suddenly director Gniech appears. He begins to speak. He wants us to return to work. He promises talks. Another director also addresses the crowd from the top of the digger. Behind the director Lech Wałęsa now appears. "Do you recognize me?" he asks. "I've been working for ten years in the shipyard and feel that I am still a shipyard worker because I've got a mandate of the confidence of the crews ... We're now beginning a sit-in strike," Wałęsa shouts to the crowd. "Hurray," comes the cry from all sides and it echoes around the yard.'

From the biography: 'As a result of the strike action, all the workshops at Gdańsk where Lech Wałęsa used to work expressed the wish to re-employ him.'

On the second day of the strike the managing director of the shipyard, Clement Gniech, signed the following document: 'In connection with the undertaking given by Citizen Lech Wałęsa that he will observe the work regulations, the directorate of the Gdańsk Lenin Shipyard enrols the citizen to work as from 15 August 1980 in his capacity of electrical engineer in the Transport Section, in grade IX in the scale of emoluments.' Underneath was an annotation: 'Continuity of employment recognized.'

From the biography: 'At present Lech Wałęsa as leader of a trade union ten million strong is opposed to all forces aiming at confrontation with the government.'

Chapter 2

Lech Wałęsa – the Man Who Spoke Up

Bolesław Fac

I want to understand the Wałęsa phenomenon. I think I can do so only through my personal observations. I have been employed at the Lenin shipyard in Gdańsk for thirty years. Since my literary debut in 1957, I have written, and published, more than a dozen volumes of poetry and prose. I have lived in Gdańsk since 1946, and I started my family here in 1958.

As I said, I have been working in the shipyard since 1950. And in those thirty years my voice has been taken from me several times. I am one of those who became silent. I was deprived of my voice just as each one of you was, just as we all were, you all were. Nothing new about that. It's happening everywhere. To many of us, in many places. We're not speechless – we're mute. We've had our voices taken away from us.

Just as writers have, for example. And workers and peasants, too, and tradesmen – a United Front of Mutes. The 'working intelligentsia' is particularly mute, since fear follows it on the wings of imagination. They've got jobs and they've got families to look after. People look on the 'technical intelligentsia' as the recruiting office providing the 'officers of production', those who give the orders ... By the end of the seventies even they had no stomach for orders, commands or the mumbling at conferences. They became aware of the extent of their helplessness in even the most blatant matters. From their vantage point 'on top' they could see even more clearly how intentions and plans and projects were disintegrating into nothingness. Their silence stemmed, therefore, from their helplessness. They started to treat their work as just a 'job down the factory'. They didn't even want 'another Poland', they didn't want to 'grow in strength', they didn't believe that 'there'll be a better life soon' ...*

So did anyone speak? Bureaucrats did, sometimes, mostly government officials – and political leaders always did. And journalists, too, of course, especially when they were waving the white rags of surrender. What about actors? After all, actors deal with the voice in a general sense. Recently, however, even they were speaking more quietly, it seemed. It's an occupational hazard: if the text doesn't speak for itself, then the actor becomes silent, too.

Naturally we mustn't forget about the repressions. Whenever anyone wanted to speak, wanted to speak using his own voice, from within, wanted to speak in his own name and in the name of others, there were repressions. Yes, quite. So all that was left was a protest coming from a solidarity of muteness, an indifference to what was being uttered in their name. The utterances became longer and made less and less sense – it was all simply very long and very boring. Even television went stupid with all that drivel it was showing. People drivelling in empty halls even though exhausted people were sitting there, dozing; drivelling in empty stadiums even though people had been rounded up to fill them; drivelling in empty rooms with the television in the corner of the family home talking to no one but the four walls. And the walls said nothing in reply. That's how we all became mute.

That morning my colleagues and I were all moved by the sight of a group of people carrying a small banner with a modest slogan. There were about twenty, thirty or maybe even fifty of them going past the windows of our office, past the library and the workshop. They aroused a lively interest in us, a fear mixed with admiration and hope. Hope of what? Maybe ... Maybe those people were going to express something in our name, in my name, something which we – I, too – haven't the courage to express. And maybe nothing was going to happen to them ... How is that possible? Well, the workers do have power. They are more numerous – they have more right to speak.

---

* All catch-phrases from the Gierek administration.

When they returned, there were many more of them: two, three, maybe as many as five hundred people. And as they went past us, they chanted their chorus:

'COME WITH US!'

The first vital sentence: the first voice calling for our support, calling for solidarity. 'Come with us! Come with us!' Just as, in 1968, the students had called to the workers who were coming out of the shipyard at the end of their shift. Just as that crowd of students had gathered outside the students' club, and outside the Press Club, and had chanted: 'Come with us!' They'd shouted it to the passers-by and many people joined them. But even more went straight past, to their homes, minding their own business. Many of them thought this was just another student prank. They recalled the year when the slogan for the student rag day had been the stirring word: 'ARSE'. This time, the words used to shock people were: 'THE PRESS LIES'. That's how it was then.

'Come with us! Come with us!' That had been the chant in December 1970 when the crowd of dockers marched from the New Port, down Jan of Koln Street, and outside the shipyard's gates. But the shipyard workers were no longer there. They had gone out earlier, through another gate, before the dockers had reached the shipyard. They went past the shipyard, past the construction offices, past the administrative buildings, the schools, the libraries and the churches ... 'COME WITH US! COME WITH US!' they'd shouted to the clerks, the architects, the pupils, the librarians, the priests, the musicians (as they had passed the conservatory they heard scales being practised on a trumpet), and to the passers-by ... Some people did join them. Later, many more swelled the several-thousand-strong crowd in the Third of May Square. 'COME WITH US!' changed to 'WE'RE WITH YOU!' We were together at last – all together. We may have been attacked, but in that innumerable throng we started discovering our strength. We knew then that we were strong, we could feel that strength as we faced the large squad of riot police. Yes, a large squad, but how small in comparison. And somewhere in that crowd of several thousand which was resisting their attacks was someone whom only his closest mates knew – I don't even know if he was leading his mates – someone who was already prepared to work on behalf of all those who were locked up in prison in the night. 'COME WITH US!' That was the first lesson in speech. The first cry of courage. And the first success.

But ten years later Wałęsa was to say that he feels he was to blame, he it was who had led the shipyard workers out on to the streets. Was it by that gate there that it happened, by that historic gate where the first victims fell? Could it have crossed his mind even then, when he was one of the crowd outside the public utility buildings in Swierczewski Street, next to the prison on Strzelecka Street, that he had the temperament of a leader? They said that he avoided the use of force, that he was an advocate of 'methods', of cunning rather than strength. So much so, in fact, that he caught the crowd completely by surprise; people who knew him were so bewildered they started throwing stones when he appeared in a first-floor window until they recognized him. They stopped as soon as they recognized his voice, as soon as they heard him say:
'IT'S ME, LADS – IT'S ME.'
'Hooray! It's Leszek!' It was like a fairy tale, a story. David had conquered Goliath. Is that when it started? When he heard their cheer? Maybe that was when he first tasted fame, his first taste of success. Maybe it was then that he became convinced that you don't always need to use force, that even the most brutish, the blindest power can be curbed, can be defeated using the right 'method'. Some people call it cunning, others call it intelligence. But afterwards he would be tormented by conscience because it had ended so tragically. After all, to begin with it had been just a game, almost like children throwing stones at the boys next door. The atmosphere prevailing at the time can best be exemplified by telling how the crowd was making its way to the prison and the police station. They were just going past the squads of riot police grouped along the railway viaduct. The police were armed to the teeth. As they went past them, the shipyard workers shouted cheerfully to the policemen: 'Come with us! You don't earn too much, either.' But the riot police were in no mood for jokes. One of them replied saying: 'We're going to have to clear out the slops someone else is preparing.' And it really wasn't a great banquet. You soon lost your appetite for it. The gas made you feel sick, and the flames burned your throat.

And afterwards, the passing years brought forgetfulness. Home, work, home, work, home, work ... In the shipyards attempts to buy people off with higher earnings and bonuses became more and more frequent since there was no other argument left. In the first May Day parade after December 1970, the shipyard workers carried a banner demanding that their dead be honoured. On the first anniversary, and for the first few years, the victims were still honoured officially. Wreaths were laid at selected cemeteries by representatives of the workers, the managements, and by political and union officials. As the years passed, this gesture became just that – a hollow, official, bureaucratic gesture. In time the anniversary was banned, the laying of wreaths was forbidden.

The mid-seventies saw the start of the familiar troubles. There was no money left for more rises and, worse still, there were no goods produced to cover them. People started to be aware. And then came June 1976. After the disastrously mismanaged price increase on basic foodstuffs, the whole of industrial Poland was gripped by strikes. The day after the parliamentary session at which the price rises were agreed unanimously, a crowd of people in their working clothes gathered round the management offices of the shipyard. We had grown adept at counting after December 1970: we made the number now about three or four thousand. The representatives of the authorities arrived: the works director, the deputy president of the province, and the secretary of the Party's Provincial Committee were all there. The officials could find no common language with the crowd; each one of them falls silent in turn. The last to leave the field of debate is the director. It is proving very difficult to get talks started at this spontaneous mass rally. Instead of conversation, threats are exchanged. Eventually, one of the workers jumps up on to an electric cart and says: 'Shipyard workers! Hull-fitters, welders, paint-sprayers, plumbers and you, too, members of the intelligentsia – listen to me!' Applause. A sociologist is standing next to me. He takes special evening classes for members of the management in his spare time. Now I hear him say: 'That man's talking as if he had a textbook. He convinced me with that "members of the intelligent-sia".' Meanwhile, the young worker speaks briefly but very much to the point. He demands that prices be brought back to the previous level and if they're not, he says, 'there'll be strikes tomorrow'. Applause. There is a general conviction that the threat will be carried through if the demand is rejected (nowadays, they call it 'strike preparedness'). Nobody's listening to the director. I couldn't place that man's face at the time. Afterwards, I learned that in fact it was Wałęsa. His words were meaningful, he showed a respect for his listeners, he found just the right motivation for action, and so on and so forth. Indeed, he did sound as if he were a textbook himself. And that

ELECTRIC CART

was to become something of a symbol later, in August 1980. If there was a museum of the working-class movement in the shipyard, instead of a room with the models of the ships built in the yard, then that old, battered, chipped, rather dirty battery-propelled cart, with its peeling paint, that ELECTRIC CART, normally used in the shipyard to distribute such trivial things as coffee, crates of soda water and so on, that cart would take its place in that museum. It had already played its part in December 1970. It was to prove a valuable factor during August 1980. It was to become a mobile platform for Lech Wałęsa.

But to return to 14 August 1980. The group of shipyard workers, swollen long since, has reached No. 2 Gate ('COME WITH US!'). That march, more than two kilometres, through the sections lying on its route, has made the group swell into a crowd of a couple of thousand – more or less as many as in 1976. All those who found themselves at the historic No. 2 Gate on that day saw each of the speakers climb up on an excavator left abandoned between some buildings. But eleven o'clock came and went, so did twelve – and even the most fiery speeches can start to pall after a time. They are sitting there – but nobody is coming out to them. The authorities, remembering the lessons of 1976, are in no hurry to meet them. People with business to attend to in the administration block just go straight past the men: in other words, so-called life just carries on. I turned to one of the workers, an acquaintance, and said: 'Nothing will come of this, will it? Not today, anyway.' And his reply was: 'Wałęsa's climbed in over the shipyard wall. If I know him, it's not going to finish that soon.'

He was right. Soon the loudspeakers of the internal radio system were switched on. Everything became louder. Voices became clearer. And, more and more, was the WORD. We began to distinguish the individual heroes of the talks. A dialogue. Conduct a dialogue – that's what they call it. At the time, though, it was a series of monologues, really. Speeches made at one another. The shipyard administration speechifying at the strikers, at the people sitting by their desks, at the people standing by their motionless machines. The strike leaders, one leader – in fact, Lech Wałęsa – speechifying at the administration, or, more accurately, the director of the shipyard. Sharp retorts, convoluted arguments, accusatory words, conciliatory phrases. Irony and anger. Anxiety and doubt. Fear and insolence. Demands and helplessness, to be joined later by threats and terror.

EQUAL AT THE VERY LEAST

The administration's representatives keep breaking off the talks more and more often for consultations in their offices. The Deputy Prime Minister is sitting in the director's office wielding powers which Wałęsa and the strikers don't know the extent of. The director has exhausted the jurisdiction he had; exhausted it as early as Friday. He'd been prepared to give everyone a pay rise by way of compensation. Not 2,000 złotys a month, that's for sure, but maybe a thousand. Wałęsa suggested, by way of a compromise, that they give us 1,500 a month extra, and that's where it stands. It would cost millions of złotys and the director would have to pay for it out of the shipyard's production. It was also said, or at least that's what the workers were telling each other, that the Deputy Prime Minister had brought a case full of money with him and that he was going to buy people off. The talks continued, with interruptions. By then everyone was out on strike, even those who were most afraid, because, when all's said and done, everyone was willing to accept 'this cost-of-living bonus'.

The talks go on. The strikers gather round the loudspeakers. At the start of each round, Wałęsa is relaxed and charming, playing his part like an old trouper. But as soon as the talks start in earnest, he becomes firm and unyielding. Each new round brings fresh attempts from the administration's representatives to fudge the issue. The director still has a lot of power at his command, for although his influence is diminishing (the workforce is listening to someone else now, not him), he can still rely on 'external forces' to restore order. This needn't be done by recourse to the agencies of 'law and order'; it can be done, for example, by replacing the management of the works, or by changing the political or union leadership. According to some, that might have been enough to satisfy the rebellious workforces. But the central Party authorities either lacked the imagination to think of that or were unwilling to put it into practice. Or, maybe, they were quite simply paralysed, immobilized by the complicated network of interrelationships existing within the Establishment.

The force which Wałęsa and the strikers could call upon is moral strength, and the support of the entire workforce. This was becoming more and more apparent. Solidarity. At the time, the only thing that word meant was that we would sit there for as long as it took Wałęsa to negotiate, to wrest, the best conditions before calling off the strike. 'He is an equal partner at the very least with the director and his advisers ...' said one of the engineers. This compliment seems to be a truism today, when Wałęsa has the wisest heads in the country around him. But in those days he was on his own, a skilled worker, an expert at fixing electric cables, at turning electricity on and off – not at turning the other kind of power out. Later we were to learn that he'd polished his debating skills at numerous works tribunals, arbitration tribunals and appeal tribunals where he had stubbornly demanded the rights he'd been deprived of by those who flouted the law. And now, there in the shipyard, during the debates about the workers' rights, feeling the workers' support, he brought his arguments out into the open and he was able to express them: he had learned his lesson well.

So Wałęsa is quite cheerful, almost, and you can't detect any sign of tiredness in his voice, though he keeps reminding the director that they're losing time. 'He is equal at the very least.' Even now you can sense the pride of the people in their leader. For that's what he is now. That's what he's become. He proved it by speaking out. By speaking for everyone. And, by doing so, he silenced those who had been distorting words for years.

Lech Wałęsa's abilities, the power of his arguments, have been witnessed before, by the people who came to No. 2 Gate in December 1979. On the anniversary of 16 December 1970, despite the fact that the day had been declared an 'energy day' in the shipyard (that is, a day off work because of 'temporary troubles with the supply of energy'), about seven thousand people had assembled by the gate. To avoid arrest, Wałęsa had been brought to the meeting in a container.* It was then, I think, that he mentioned his sense of almost personal responsibility for the first time. He spoke about how, nine years earlier, he had led 'his colleagues out on to the streets'. And then he ended by swearing that he would do everything to get a monument built there, in the very place where the shipyard's first victims had fallen. Or maybe he was talking about a commemorative plaque ... No – it was a monument. He told every single person to return the following year bringing a stone in each pocket. 'We'll build a mound with those stones, we'll cement them over, and that will be our monument. We'll erect it ourselves.'

Saturday, 16 August 1980. The director promises to put up a plaque. Did he have his superiors' permission to give the workers that promise, I wonder. His proposal is that it could, perhaps, be put up somewhere in the shipyard. 'No, we must have a monument,' is the strikers' reply. 'All right,' says the director, 'a monument is quite feasible.' However, now it is obvious that he is not in a position to make a decision like that. Maybe he does believe that the authorities will consent to putting up a monument in the shipyard. Nobody knows what Wałęsa thought of it all at the time, and there's not much point asking him about it now. After all, the monument is there, outside the gate, as high as the neighbouring buildings, taller than the public buildings nearby.

But I'm sure that people aren't even thinking about a monument like that at the moment. The first task is to survive these eighteen days in one piece; the first task is to win this shipyard strike. Then the threads of solidarity with the other, smaller plants will need to be drawn together patiently, the plants which will be crushed without the support of the large, the huge works. Some of the authorities' representatives make no attempt to conceal their cynicism. 'Let the big fish sign,' they're saying, 'and we'll sort out the small fry.' Apparently there had even been a phone call to the Urban Transport Establishment threatening the use of violence against them.

The negotiations went on from Thursday to Saturday. The

* This version does not quite accord with the account given above by Florian Wiśniewski (see p. 42).

weather on that Saturday, 17 August, was good. In fact, it was too fine a day. The weekend looked very enticing: anglers, allotment owners, hikers, walkers – all longed for days like this. 'If only that Wałęsa would call it a day,' people were saying. 'Why doesn't he just take what he's got? It's a great success as it is.' All watched, knowing that the strike was drawing to a close, they waited by the gate, by the loudspeakers, for the end to be announced. At last: 'I announce that the strike is over. We'll meet at work on Monday.' Relief. Wałęsa, off-key as usual, starts up the National Anthem. He's no singer, some of them were saying. He certainly knows how to talk, though, others riposted. True enough, they all agreed; he's done us proud.

Most of us went home. That was when the worst moments started for Wałęsa. He has never liked to talk about them. The situation had caught him unawares; it had happened outside the building of the conference hall. There was a platform there with a microphone and loudspeakers. We called it the 'political disco'. Anyone could get up there and say what they wanted. You could even recite poetry. In fact, that's what one fellow did; they couldn't pull him away from the microphone. And it was there, too, that a delegate from the transport base in Oliwa spoke from. The workers in Oliwa wanted to join the strike, but they didn't know what they were supposed to do. Neither did their delegate. He stood there, looking round helplessly. At the same time as Wałęsa was about to bring the strike to a close in the health and safety building, outside the representative of the transport workers was being bundled up on to the platform. He stood at the microphone and had his say. It ended with a plea for support for the transport workers. Moments later the tram-drivers came out of the hall and joined us. The platform was surrounded by young men – a hundred, two hundred, maybe even five hundred young boys. 'Solidarity! Solidarity! Solidarity!' Another group of about twenty young men went over to the windows of the conference hall and started chanting: 'Two thousand! Two thousand! Two thousand!', casting doubt on the acceptability of the concessions made during negotiations. It must be stated quite clearly that all this had been organized from outside the shipyard. The shipyard workers were quite satisfied with what Wałęsa had negotiated. At the same time, however, they did not see the end of the strike and victory within the framework of a narrow and sectarian self-interest. There was a general feeling that the terms negotiated for the shipyard would serve as a model for other plants in Gdańsk, and that we should find out before Monday what the authorities' real intentions were and what was the real strength of the strikers in Gdańsk and Gdynia. On Monday we would have been ready to strke again to support, for example, the tram-drivers.

When he came out of the hall, one glance was enough to convince Wałęsa that the shipyard workers' strike could not end like that. And so the threads which might have snapped, the fabric which might have been torn to tatters by Monday was immediately seized and kept in one piece. He accepted the situation with the words:

'WE ARE STRIKING, AREN'T WE?'

The question was a rhetorical one, even though there were no more than a thousand people left on the field of battle. That Saturday night and Sunday morning were hard for those who remained in the shipyard. Afterwards we were told that there hadn't been enough people left to man all the sentry posts along the gates and walls. Things improved on Sunday, when part of the workforce returned. But before that happened, Wałęsa had to drink his cup of bitterness. Graffiti saying: 'Wałęsa is a traitor!' appeared on the walls during the night. That same Saturday afternoon, two lady 'emissaries', sent from the Gdańsk shipyard, had spoken in the repair yard. They had attacked the Gdańsk shipyard workers angrily for 'getting their settlement and running'; invectives flew and Wałęsa was savaged. The 'emissaries'' intemperate language made the repair yard workers suspicious, and when the talks with Deputy Prime Minister Pyka were in progress, this unfortunate incident would be brought up frequently. There was a general consensus of opinion that the outburst had stopped the repair workers from joining the shipyard just when they were ready to do so. There is no doubt that the two ladies' intentions had been noble, but their anger and bitterness had proved poor counsellors. The way that speeches are made is a matter of some importance, too.

Wałęsa would never use language like that against anyone, at any time or in any situation. That is one more characteristic of his speeches, that even his sharpest language never insulted his audience, and even his most violent speeches were such that anyone could listen to them. He never used invective or insults. It has to be put down to his refinement, not forgetting his close ties with the Christian ethic.

Because the masses won't be moved by curses or insults. For a good few days the repair workers did not trust us. Not because we had left the yard on Saturday, but because we hadn't come to them with

THE RIGHT WORDS.

On Sunday, 17 August, Wałęsa took a wooden cross on to his shoulders, like Simon of Cyrene, carried it out through the gate and put it on the spot where the monument would be erected in the future. The cross was cemented in, and in this way the unity of several hundred striking works – the shipyard, various factories, institutions, offices, associations and unions – would be cemented throughout the next two weeks of the joint strike ... The graffiti against Wałęsa were wiped off during Sunday night, and that same night Wałęsa formally took over as head of the committee which had been formed as an act of solidarity to protect the interests of the works in Gdańsk, Gdynia, Elbląg, Tczew, Pruszcz, Lębork and many others.

As late as Monday morning, the director, who had signed the shipyard's agreement with Wałęsa on Saturday, tries to appeal to the loyalty of the workforce. He accuses Wałęsa of going back on his word. Wałęsa concedes the point. 'That leaflet of yours,' he says, 'is the best thing you've done here.' And then he adds, sarcastically: 'What a pity you didn't put your name on it.' Good-humoured with just a touch of malice. The director shrugs. 'It's not my problem any more. This isn't a shipyard strike. It's a strike of solidarity.' Yes, I think it was the director who was the first to use the phrase:

A STRIKE OF SOLIDARITY.

But they have been robbed of the opportunity to use the internal radio network to make announcements, appeals and speeches. Before the 'technical troubles' occurred, the director had had just enough time to make his appeal to the workforce. Then he fell silent. The workforce has become deaf to his cries, anyway.

The crowd does not believe that there's a fault in the radio network. They insist that the director give them access to the transmitter. The director is helpless, but the crowd doesn't know that. 'Wałęsa, Wałęsa, Wałęsa.' Several thousand people standing, or sitting, outside the management building start chanting. From now on, this chant will be repeated again and again, alternating with the chant of: 'Leszek, Leszek, Leszek!' He can do everything, he must want to do everything, Wałęsa knows everything. Leszek's capabilities are unlimited.

A myth, a legend, renown. This naïve faith stems, no doubt, from the fact that, by his personality, with his words and views, he has managed to cement together what had been fragmented, what had seemed so difficult to gather into one entity. What had been dwarfed was beginning to grow, what had crawled before was beginning to get wings. Ambiguous phrases were giving way to ceremonious incantations, simplicity was being given an accompaniment of an emotional melody. Wałęsa gathered a crowd outside the building, not for the first time – but this was the first time that there was no fear. The crowd was growing in courage. The strength emanating from this crowd can be sensed, it's almost tangible as it flows from one person to another – and it doesn't suspect for a moment that its potential might be limited.

Wałęsa is to arrange with the director for the radio to be put back into operation and at the strikers' disposal. He makes his way up to the first floor for 'talks'. A few people already know that there is nothing the director can do, that it's simply not possible for him to do anything about the radio. Maybe he is already utterly helpless: maybe someone else is already taking the decisions. In which case even a hundred Wałęsas won't help. But the crowd still believes that Wałęsa will get things fixed. So Wałęsa is being put through this test, too; this second test of his capabilities. I watch him closely when he returns; he's grim-faced. How is he going to explain his defeat to them? This thing can't fall apart over arguments about one man's capabilities, surely, or about the limits of decision-making in the shipyard. He gets up on to the electric cart and silences the crowd with that familiar gesture of his. 'Listen to me. I couldn't do it. No, no, no – I couldn't.' (A terrifying silence descends. All eyes are fixed on the face of our leader.) 'I went to the director and demanded access to the transmitters. He put his hands up – like this – and said: "Mr Wałęsa, you can do what you like with me, arrest me – but I can't. There's nothing I can do ..."' At this point, Wałęsa's voice took on a dramatic tone. 'Do you think I can arrest anyone? I, who have been arrested so often myself, who was put under arrest just as my wife was going into labour? No, no – I can't.' And, that said, he covered his eyes with his hand, like an actor, as if the very thought of such a deed could blind him. 'Could I have done it? Tell me, is that what you wanted me to do?' 'No, no,' the assembled crowd responds in chorus.

Was it sheer skill, or had he really been so deeply affected by the director's simple gesture? What matters is that he has passed this latest examination. He has preserved his

AUTHORITY

intact in the face of its most demanding opponent, in the face of a crowd that worships him.

Another scene. Gdańsk television had interviewed the director; during the interview, the window of his room had been open. Outside, the crowd had been clapping a speaker on the platform, and the clapping merged with the director's words, making it seem that it was his words that were being applauded (it's hard to tell now if it was just pure coincidence or the result of skilful editing). But the crowd wants to hear the tape of the interview. Having heard it, it wants the tape wiped. Taught by television's past habits, the people don't trust the reporters. The television technician claims that he can't wipe bits of the recording without damaging other vital fragments as well. Technically speaking, he's right; but morally, the crowd is right. Like the rest of Polish television, Gdańsk television has, in the past, given ample evidence of its ability to distort situations like this in order to manipulate reality into something much less real. The dispute is boiling up into a full-scale row, the reporter is in danger of losing his equipment and, feeling threatened, is defending himself. 'Let Wałęsa decide,' says one of the bystanders. The crowd starts chanting: 'Wałęsa, Leszek, Wałęsa, Leszek.' It's some time before Wałęsa appears. They've dragged him out of the conference hall where he was taking a short nap, hoping to refresh himself. As always, he gets up on to the cart. 'Tell us, Leszek, is that programme, is that recording okay to be put out?' Wałęsa listens to a fragment of the tape. The crowd waits for his verdict with quiet concentration. Eventually, only those who are standing nearest to him know at what precise moment, Wałęsa grimaces as if he were being forced to swallow some nasty medicine. Then, with a scowl of distaste, he pushes the apparatus away (Get thee behind me, Satan of technology! *Apage Satanas!*). The crowd roars with joy – it is the reply they've been expecting. Leszek jumps down from the cart and, without taking any notice of the applause, indeed, almost seeming to be slightly irritated by it ('fancy waking me for something as trivial as that'), he crosses rapidly to the conference hall building. Today I wonder if his verdict was just. And did it need to be? How could it have hurt the reporter? What did he put on the other side of the scales – the honesty of journalists?

But there were some
SUBLIME MOMENTS.
There was that day, about half-way through the strike, about half-way through the first week of the solidarity strike ... The sky was a leaden grey. Rain was forecast. The day was chilly and grey. People were huddling in corners, trying to keep warm. The North Yard and the repair yard were still persevering with their 'whimsy', conducting 'their own' 'individual' talks with Pyka,* by-passing the MKS (Interworks Strike Committee), even though they were in sympathy with us, and even though both yards were right next to the Gdańsk shipyard. By that time there were already over four hundred works united in the MKS. At about nine in the morning we heard a call through the loudspeakers: 'We're going to the repair yard.' From nowhere, it seemed, about a couple of thousand people collected round the battered electric cart. Unfortunately, though, the talks in the repair yard produced no results. The procession returns, crossing the pontoon bridge and moving towards the wall of the North Yard. A man with great faith in electronics tries to dissuade us from going there. 'Leszek,' he says, 'there's no point. What we need to do is get some loudspeakers round the perimeter of the yard and transmit the talks to them.' 'Human contact is what counts,' says Wałęsa, gravely. 'People have got to talk to each other. That's what matters most. And that's how we'll do it.'

---

*Tadeusz Pyka, a Deputy Prime Minister, was the first leader of the government negotiating team at Gdańsk. But his policy of dividing the strike movement by negotiating separately with each enterprise failed, and on 21 August he was recalled and replaced by Mieczysław Jagielski.

The cart, with Wałęsa atop, rolls on, propelled by the battery, or maybe simply pushed by the young workers who are shouting, chanting: 'Leszek – Freedom – Leszek – Freedom.' Our throats tighten with emotion. Because we know we are, we really are at last, that's what we can be like, ourselves, me, him, her, yourself ... Eventually our voices can be heard raised high above us quite naturally, not hiding our feelings, unafraid of lofty words. It neither surprises nor shocks us to see the young men kissing the cart which Wałęsa is using. He's their own Leszek. We accept it as a natural gesture of thanks; with this gesture they elevate their leader above themselves because he has given them strength, they have risen above the crowd with him because they are at the head of the procession with him. And Leszek is radiant, though tired; a straightforward man, though no less fascinating for that.

That's how we are when we arrive at the cement wall separating the two shipyards, where talks between the two neighbours begin. Wałęsa argues in favour of solidarity, unity, the necessity to combine all our efforts to achieve common aims. His words, though listened to attentively, seem to be coming up against an invisible barrier standing between them and us. It's beginning to look as if things are going to end the same way as they did in the repair yard. There were no particularly striking similarities between us. They didn't have their own Wałęsa, and in fact that was one reason why the people who sat idly on the walls, or who stood, or sat, by their motionless pieces of apparatus, were more malleable. Even their organization to provide food supplies for the men was woefully inadequate. The strikers in the North Yard were, quite simply, hungry. 'It's all very well for you men in the Gdańsk shipyard – you're in the public eye. The townspeople come to you and they bring you grub.' And it was true. Thousands of people had brought us provisions as well as words of encouragement and solidarity. And in addition we did have a canteen which served us basic meals.

And so this conversation between the hungry and the well-fed continued, a conversation between the self-confident and the people tormented by their own inferiority complex. Suddenly, some people from our side started handing over loaves of bread to the other side of the wall. The brown loaves passed from hand to hand, symbols of our solidarity with them, gifts of brotherhood extended to those who were with us, who should have been with us. Our daily bread – THE STRIKERS' COMMUNION – a loaf of dry bread.

Fortunately, August 1980 was a warm month and, as long as it didn't rain, our 'lodgings' weren't too much of a torture. People slept anywhere: on floors, the grass, asphalt, pieces of polystyrene, inflated mattresses, tables, desks – anything. Even sleeping as they sat in their overalls on chairs arranged by the gate, facing the entrance, forming a human barricade – nothing special. Only those who were on night-duty at the gates used to sleep during the day to make up for it.

Even the greatest dangers can be taken in one's stride. Towards the end of the strike, only the members of the praesidium spent the nights in the shipyard itself: the rest of us used to go home at eleven at night. And then, on Thursday of the last week, the dispatch office intercepted a bulletin on short-wave radio which could have meant that people would start to be rounded up by the authorities. What had till then been ordinary searches for leaflets would now, it seemed, change into a full-scale round-up of all the MKS delegates. It's easy to guess what effect this news must have had on the talks which were drawing to a close, especially as, towards the end of that week, the Government Commission had begun to vacillate, becoming evasive and ambiguous.

The shipyard workers had just been getting ready for the night. It was nearly eleven o'clock and the delegates were starting to make their way home. Suddenly, someone came rushing into the hall saying that there might be a roundup. Wałęsa's 'bodyguards', who were, as a rule, very decisive, took one look at the messenger, who was almost foaming in his haste, and took him straight to the chairman. 'Leszek, there's someone here who's got some information; says it's urgent, says it can only be given to you and nobody else ...' The 'bodyguard', too, had been affected by the tension of the moment. Wałęsa was slouching in an armchair, exhausted rather than dismissive. 'It's nonsense,' he said, waving the 'report' away scornfully as soon as he'd heard it. People all around him sighed with relief. But a careful observer would have caught a wary look coming into Wałęsa's eyes. He leant across to one of the men next to him and said, softly: 'Get one delegate from each section to stay behind; they can spend the night in the hall. The rest can go home as usual.'

A young girl with a large bag appeared from the shadows. She'd come over from the gate. 'Anything happening?' 'No, nothing,' she replied calmly. 'Are the sentries on duty?' 'Yes.' 'Have they been checking people?' 'Yes, and they've been letting them out.'

Wałęsa's CALM permeated everyone there. Those were crucial moments, with the tension relaxing, and then, suddenly, rising again. How many such moments were there? Nerves of steel were needed to withstand those constant changes of tension. He must have kept a very tight hold not to give way to panic; it seemed, indeed, as if it were all developing along the lines of some well-laid plan. He said once: 'We'll sit by the gate and they can carry us out. We won't go out, we'll just sit there ...' Waiting for the outcome was no holiday and only by remaining calm could we be saved. And we were saved.

Saturday. The last moments before the initialling of the document. On the walls next to the shipyard, someone had stuck posters up attacking the government side and their leader Jagielski, thereby casting a doubt on Wałęsa's, and the MKS praesidium's, good faith. The last talks took place in the small room and were continued in the hall where the plenary assembly was sitting. The course of the talks and the result of the negotiations did not satisfy those in the hall. They feel betrayed; a radical grouping forms and makes conditions which could delay the negotiations considerably and might even break them off. The situation in the country outside isn't good, either: members of the opposition in Warsaw are still being arrested, a sombre augury for the future. Some members of the plenum demand that unequivocal assurances about the release of prisoners should be given. We can hear these discussions through the loudspeakers. The radicals' arguments appear to be winning over the majority of the assembly. Points which have already been agreed are opened up again. Wałęsa's voice struggles to be heard above the chorus of opposition. The radio technician stays cool. 'Ladies and gentlemen,' he says, 'the loudspeakers will have to be switched off. The apparatus is over-heating.' And that was certainly true.

Silence. There is silence everywhere, and it's worse. We seem to be listening to the beating of our own hearts. There is a sense of helplessness in the air, and a fear that everything will collapse, that the edifice which has been constructed over such a long period will collapse now that one matchstick has been pulled out. We've been cooped up in here far too long; we've been exposed to far too many 'signals'. The pressure of being subjected to external and internal indoctrination is beginning to take its toll. We don't want to go back to what we've just been through; we won't be able to stick it any more. We're prepared to sign any sensible compromise just as long as we can get out of here and go home. We're even prepared to leave the others, those imprisoned in Warsaw, to their own fate – for the time being, anyway. Wałęsa says: 'We'll add an appendix to the main document in which the details of how and when ...' He's right: we can't throw away our insurance, the main agreement. We can't start all over again. And yet, deep down, a lingering doubt remains. Isn't this a form of betrayal? (Meanwhile, the experts have joined in the debate in the main hall and the scales have tilted towards common sense – my God, what exactly does that mean? – and come down on the side of the moderates.) But where is Wałęsa? We need him now. Led by a kind of instinct, we make our way over to No. 2 Gate.

The silent crowd, as if terrified by what it had heard, was still standing there. Some two, maybe three thousand people waiting in the late evening for words of encouragement. Night was approaching, the last night before the signing of the agreement. They were waiting for an assurance that everything would continue on its victorious course. Meanwhile, through the loudspeakers, came voices full of anger, stoking up uncertainty. The frayed nerves of the speakers did nothing to calm ours. The crowd froze in the place where Wałęsa was wont to conduct his evening 'vespers'.

Even a walk in the cool evening air had not calmed me. But I reached the gate and started to look for someone with whom I could share my feelings of confusion, the struggle between my common sense and the moral reasons for defending those who had been imprisoned ... Then, as I was coming to the gate, I heard the crowd laughing. On our side of the gate, on the shipyard side, there was Wałęsa standing up on his cart, talking with the crowd. He wasn't firing them with a speech; he was simply conducting a conversation, a friendly chat, almost. His evening audience: the atmosphere was more like that at a picnic than a mass rally. He himself had just been through a battle which threatened to break up that beautifully constructed solidarity. Now, here, in the evening light, slightly blinded by the glare of the electric lights near the gate, Wałęsa could relax. He was at ease. In this crowd he probably found the thing which had been carrying him through those days, those weeks and years, which had made him cling on to his belief. He had the crowd's attention, the sense of oneness with it, and the sense of being able to prevail upon it by using just the right words, words which would land on the fertile ground of faith. He was pleased, therefore, to find himself face to face with the crowd which was waiting for him. In a place and at a time when others might have felt uneasy, when others might have felt tongue-tied or uncertain, he was consumed with joy. 'And now we'll all go to our homes, take a bath, go to bed and tomorrow, later, our Poland will have more citizens. And now, therefore, let us sing the National Anthem for this country of ours.' (And here he started the singing of the anthem.) Oh, and one more thing: 'Let us sing a religious song to God because now we can't go any further without God ...'

I was grateful to him for that Saturday evening, just before the night preceding the last day of the strike, the day when peace between Poles was signed. Thanks to him I was able to sleep, even though I was lying on the floor between a desk and a bookcase. My sleep was deep and sound. I was grateful to him for that peace of mind which, so it seemed to me then, he had rescued at the very last minute. I was grateful to him for calming my 'intellectual's' over-sensitive nerves. Isn't that sufficient reason for me to wish him all the best, to wish him well? I hope all does go well with him. May his human weaknesses, his comic gestures and phrases be forgiven him because his intentions are pure and because, so far, his are the moral rights. Because he did get up and he did speak. He spoke for me, he spoke for us – because I, because we, lacked the courage to speak.

Lech Wałęsa, that brave man, has saved our self-respect. He has done it without seeking applause and without expecting any rewards. Let's wish him well.

Gdańsk, May 1981

Chapter 3

Growing

Andrzej Drzycimski

To write about a public figure who is still alive and around whom a legend or even a cloud of mystery and innuendo has already grown is not only difficult but risky. With such a figure there are no problems with documentary materials; there are many people ready to supply some new details to assist characterization. The author's problem is how to write about him: in adulatory fashion, or debunking him? To adopt the role of a judge who carries the burden of his knowledge and the power of passing sentence, or to become a sycophantic panegyrist? Even if one attempts to be completely objective, by some people one would be called a hagiographer, by others an iconoclast.

Such were the disquieting views with which I received a proposal from Maritime Publications to participate in a collective work on Wałęsa. I thought of the various forms my contribution could take; each seemed to be unsuitable, too general. I decided to make a personal statement consisting of my own reflections and observations.

I don't feel any lack of materials; quite the contrary. My own home archives contain tapes of statements by Wałęsa, a considerable number of notes of conversations with him, photographs, articles and other interviews. But it is difficult to write about a man one has known well since the hectic days of the Gdańsk strike in August 1980, when one has written about many of his public appearances, interviewed him and has gone with him on his first two foreign journeys. My uneasiness is the greater because we lack the historical perspective necessary for a sober presentation of 'the Wałęsa phenomenon'. One cannot yet unravel the whole complexity of this phenomenon. We lack facts not only about Wałęsa, but about the wider issue, the birth of the strikers' solidarity, and later of the union Solidarity. Not only can we not understand the Wałęsa phenomenon without them, we cannot understand ourselves either.

Lech Wałęsa is a child of our times – restless, tempestuous, often unable to make unequivocal decisions. He is the personification of the younger generation of socialist Poland. It is a mature generation, spontaneous in its reactions but sensible. Firm, but at the same time ready for dialogue and compromise. With ambitious aims, yet reasonable in its attitudes to country and state. A generation that is not very receptive to officially launched doctrines, and mistrustful of empty declarations and senseless slogans. A generation quite knowledgeable of general subjects, but lacking a full knowledge of the system under which it lives. It is a generation that does not remember the Stalinist days and did not participate in the Polish October of 1956; but it is a generation whose childhood and youth were affected by the events of March 1968 and the tragic December 1970, some of them indeed having of their own free will participated in these events.* They later lived through the drama of frustrated hopes aroused by the early seventies and dashed by the collapse of 1976.

Lech Wałęsa grew up in People's Poland. He has experienced his country's most dramatic moments. He did not flinch, but participated in them. He grew by acquiring experience – not at second hand, but his own. He had, as a child needs to touch things, to assess matters for himself in order to form his own opinion. Instinctively he was searching for his own direction. At first he was unsure precisely what he was seeking. He simply liked tackling problems that others considered hopeless. These experiences enlarged his interest in the needs of others. Later came his transformation into someone who would serve an idea which became the passion of his life. Until August 1980 he was unknown

---

* In October 1956, Poland threw off direct Soviet tutelage and destroyed the remains of the Stalinist dictatorship. In March 1968, as the 'Prague Spring' began to blossom in Czechoslovakia, student riots in Warsaw, Kraków and elsewhere were repressed by the police, and a ruthless purge was launched against the liberal intellectuals. The 'tragic December' refers to the strikes and rioting in the Baltic ports in that month.

to the wider public, but while the strike at Gdańsk was in progress, a legend began to grow around him and this has now lifted him to the pantheon of national mythology. On this pedestal he occupies a considerable place. Without undue modesty one can state that history will undoubtedly keep that place for him whatever may happen to him in the future.

From the beginning of the Gdańsk strike, I have observed its course: at first outside No. 2 Gate of the Lenin shipyard, later mingling for a fortnight, from early in the morning until late at night, with the delegates of the striking workers. At the very centre of events one tends to react to them very subjectively; thus I tried to become immersed in the prevailing mood of the strikers, to absorb everything they spoke about.

It was during the first days that I noticed on the other side of the shipyard gate a bewhiskered man who often spoke in a hoarse voice. I was told that this was Wałęsa, the chairman of the strike committee. He spoke simply. In short sentences he described the situation. When I found myself at last inside the shipyard, I saw him both in the hall with the delegates and when he spoke to smaller groups about the continuing uncertainty and lack of response from the government representatives. In these conditions I found an opportunity to ask him a few questions about the steps that the MKS (Interworks Strike Committee) would take. He was quite firm: 'We shall not yield, we want free unions.'

His authority amongst the strikers was unshakeable. He often also spoke at No. 2 Gate when the crowd assembled in front of it was calling for him, looking for him: 'Le-szek! Le-szek!' He spoke to the delegates of the workshops that were also on strike. In tense situations he smiled a lot. He was under strain yet relaxed. When he felt that those on both sides of the gates and those in the hall were supporting him, he would flatten his thick hair and smooth down his sweeping moustache. He would raise both arms with fists clenched, to greet the assembled crowd. When leaving, he raised both hands with fingers spread to form the letter 'V'. His improvised speeches delighted the crowds. He encouraged them to hold on, to be stubborn but cautious. Fre-quently, when a serious incident occurred, he grabbed the loudspeaker and sang the Polish National Anthem, and at No. 2 Gate he sometimes added to the anthem 'God who hast saved Poland . . .'

One felt that in a crowd he was in his element. This is why we listened with great attention to his pronouncements that were directed straight at us, the assembled journalists. These were the nightly mini-press conferences when, exhausted to the limits of human endurance, after a whole day of tension, of waiting, of discussions and declarations, hoarse or even ill, he would revive when somebody asked him a question connected with the current situation. He answered briefly, concisely. He stressed his sentences by the expression on his face, the tone of his voice and the gestures of his hands. In situations that seemed to us hopeless, he tried to leave at least a ray of hope. We were, however, only listeners, because there was a blockade of information around the strikers. This lasted almost until the end of the strike. For him we were not the people able to describe what was really happening. Foreign journalists who flocked to the shipyard were in a different position. In the final period, over 200 of them passed through the yard. They arrived with Polish accreditations, from other socialist countries, and also, because of visa difficulties, as 'tourists'. They were the ones whom he addressed most willingly. He knew that what he told them would be included in the dispatches of the world press agencies' information services on the same day. From these messages Poland learned what was happening at the time in the Three Cities (Gdańsk, Gdynia and Sopot) and in other Polish towns.

When speaking, Wałęsa reacted spontaneously, but at the same time with great feeling for any given situation. This was so for instance on 21 August, when after a flood of articles in the press, especially in Warsaw newspapers, about 'the men who direct the strike' he broached that subject in front of the delegates. He said: 'Ladies and gentlemen. I would like to state my position in several matters. If someone observes the development of events, he should notice certain facts. I notice them. I've wondered whether to mention them or not, but have come to the conclusion that perhaps . . . I should mention them. First of all: we were accused at the beginning – and that was a hook on which we were to hang, yes, this is true, we were dangling from it – KOR (Committee for the

Defence of the Workers),* the Movement of Young Poland, political opposition. This was a little wedge, a good little wedge. Because it's known that just those organizations, in spite of their being ... in spite of their not being amongst us, work for us. This means: that in cities – where they exist – they transmit and work. And now, because of this, the authorities have allowed themselves to disarm all those activists. Can we blame them? When they work for us?!'

Voices from the hall: 'No, no, no.'

Wałęsa: 'Therefore I declare officially that if the authorities don't stop arresting the activists of KOR and other social and political organizations, no negotiations will take place. NONE! (Applause, calls of 'Bravo'.) They've tried to entice us, are enticing us now and will continue to do so! We've been waiting for a week for them, but they're still speculating! We are here and here they must come! As if ... we ... So that we should not clash with them! Because we'll show them how one has to deal with matters! Without cease they want blood from us! Therefore I'm warning the authorities – they must think it over. We've finished playing games! They speculate ... they don't want to let me out because I'm talking sense and I know. But we cannot get excited and indignant. There are facts and we observe these facts. (Applause.) This is why I declare once more: There must not be any arrests or house arrests of people who in effect don't lead us – because we lead ourselves – but who have helped us and earlier, a little earlier, have opened our eyes ... to history and about what we really deserve. (Applause). Yes, these are exceptional cases, that's why ... but let's return to earth. I should like ... because there are these questions: well, yes, these free unions ... but do I know how to do it? Ladies and gentlemen, it's a fact ... again those who have been observing all those years should have realized that free unions have existed for the last two years. It's also a fact that they haven't got their statutes. But I think it's a good thing that they haven't got them, because it's we who have to work on the statutes. We must make them so that they should suit us. And therefore all these solutions – the technical ones – will be resolved,

* A political opposition group formed in 1977, originally to support workers and their families who had been the victims of repression after the strikes in Radom and Warsaw in June 1976.

because we know about them. I am also an activist of the free unions, and this is why I'm here and concerned about these matters. For if I were not here ... I'm not saying that there are persons who are irreplaceable. There are. But we've known these very matters earlier and therefore the free trade unions of the Coast are here. They're here and they act. And where are the original unions? Where is the plaenum, where are the works councils? They have deserted us! We have not deserted you! We are, and will remain, here. And the statutes will be worked out for the branches, for suitable groups, and we shall shape them so that they suit us and so that we are satisfied with them. And we are well aware of all this. We shall ask advisers who are ready to help us. And we shall do it very very quickly – so that you won't be troubled – and you should explain matters thus. Let's have freedom. Let's have the right of association. When we get this right, we shall fulfil it, but first of all, first of all let's have the right. I thank you.' (Applause.)

Such appearances, in an atmosphere of enormous tension and expectation, lifted the spirits of those who were hesitant and gave others the strength to endure. At these improvised meetings he spoke about his own programme in simple language which everyone could understand. He addressed himself to the workers. But these were workers who belied the propaganda model in which they had been cast. Those to whom he spoke were educated and knew about the latest technical advances and about the country's problems. The fact that their sensibilities, their experience, their knowledge, their ability to conduct a dialogue and appreciate the general situation in the country were not recognized made them unwilling and reluctant to subscribe to the officially voiced slogans. Those seemed insincere to them. Speaking the truth openly, even the most painful truth, was Wałęsa's main objective and trump card. It gave him an increasing authority. There was also the urgent need for a new type of solidarity and social wisdom.

A few events from that period stick in my memory: they emphasized Wałęsa's personal qualities. Among these was the moment on 21 August when the writers of the Gdańsk centre and, a day later, representatives of a group of Warsaw intellectuals gained access to Solidarity. The writers came to the shipyard gate, just as any other delegates, to present their appeal to the MKS. In the meeting hall Lech Bądkowski read the text of the appeal.* In response, there was a great ovation, everybody getting up from their seats and singing the National Anthem in unison, and a spontaneous proposal by Lech Wałęsa that Bądkowski should be elected to the presidency of the MKS. This proposal was accepted by acclamation.

During the night of 21 to 22 August, two representatives of the group of Warsaw intellectuals arrived: Tadeusz Mazowiecki, a newspaper editor, and Bronisław Geremek, a university lecturer. They brought an appeal to the presidency of the MKS. Mazowiecki recalls that it was then that he met Wałęsa, who suggested the formation of a committee of advisers which would assist the strikers. It was not known at the time how everything would end. So when Wałęsa asked how long they would remain with the strikers, the answer was: to the bitter end, whenever that was. The understanding between them was complete. The intellectuals appreciated the workers' determination and the workers saw their arrival as proof that they were fighting for a common cause. In the morning of 23 August, after Bądkowski's statement that the Kolodziejski region had that day proposed to MKS the establishment of working contacts in order to make preparations for talks with the Government Commission, Wałęsa proclaimed in his usual style that a committee of advisers had been called to life during the night. This important information was presented to the delegates in a most natural way: 'In connection with ... so that we shall all benefit – we must call into being a group of advisers. Well, we must be, in sum total, sufficiently clever and good, what? So we have done this. Were we right?' (Applause.)

When the same evening the Government Commission arrived, the crowd murmured: 'They've come.' One section of the gate was opened with difficulty by stewards and the bus containing the commission members tried to enter the shipyard. Nothing doing. The workers shouted: 'Stop,' 'Walk to meet us,' 'On your knees,' 'Get out.' The atmosphere became tense. They banged with their fists on the sides of the bus, and in front of it a compact, angry crowd of workers was massing. Somebody in front of me was

*Lech Bądkowski, a novelist from the Gdańsk region, was elected to the praesidium of the strike and became its first information officer.

struggling with the door of the bus and shouting: 'Get out!' The delegation, with the Deputy Prime Minister at its head, began to leave the bus. Their faces were pale, they were tense: an avenue was opened up before them with workers on each side. All eyes were turned on them. There was no cordiality. The news photographers, cameramen and television operators were buzzing in the crowd trying to get a true picture of that meeting. Wałęsa greeted the delegation, together with the director of the shipyard, Klemens Gniech. First talks followed at once. The crowd meanwhile started their deafening chant: 'Le-szek! Le-szek!' and Leszek himself, smiling, raised, in his characteristic gesture, his two clenched fists. The workers responded with the same, to him alone. They raised their arms and made the 'V' sign. In front of the entrance to the building of the BHP* there was a commotion caused by news photographers who wanted to get into the hall, which was next to a smaller one. A part of the government delegation suddenly found itself in that crowd of workers. They were visibly shaken. But one shout of the steward: 'Make way for the government delegation', and that angry crowd broke up the group of photographers and joined hands, making a double lane.

The delegates pass into the great hall. Here, from the platform, in the presence of all, Jagielski† greeted the members of the praesidium and, immediately afterwards, the Government Commission with their hosts went into the small room for a working session. There was a crush and a commotion. Wałęsa asked for passage and when all those present had come down from the rostrum there was applause again and the deafening chant: 'Le-szek! Le-szek!' The talks began. After Jagielski's first few sentences, the workers were disenchanted. They asked 'What has he brought us?' The discussion faltered and fundamental differences appeared. Apposite remarks of the MKS were greeted with a storm of applause in the large hall, where loudspeakers relayed what was being said in the smaller meeting hall.

Every so often Wałęsa, who watched the discussion, would utter a relevant word. He did not seem to be inhibited. He was decisive but relaxed. One could feel clearly that he knew what he wanted

* BHP stands for the Polish words for Safety and Hygiene.

† Mieczysław Jagielski, at the time a Deputy Prime Minister, led the government negotiating team in the main talks with the MKS.

to achieve. When Jagielski entered into very detailed disquisitions, Wałęsa suggested moving on to the next point: 'We shan't be able to deal with this subject. We have our point of view – we might come to a compromise later.' He toned down the demands and conditions, but did not change their essence. The conditions he treated not as the demands of the strikers but as an expression of the wishes of the whole community. In a situation where Jagielski pretended to believe that everything was in order, Wałęsa reminded him that they were meeting to 'approach the matter honestly'. They had gathered here in the name of truth, in order to lance the boil. The whole praesidium concurred with his thinking.

By the time they had come to the fifth point for consideration, the discrepancies were so great that further discussion became fruitless. The meeting that had represented all the strikers' hopes was about to be dissolved. Deadlock was complete, the more so as the initial conditions had not been agreed, namely the unblocking of telecommunications, especially with Warsaw. The government side explained its position so inanely that each statement was greeted with laughter. In order to save the meeting, which was visibly disintegrating, Wałęsa suggested that the Prime Minister's views about the twenty-one conditions should be heard without a discussion.

With a detailed enumeration – what, how much, where from, and why we import, consume and spend – Wałęsa returned, with his amazing feeling for society's susceptibilities, to the most vital matter: the cause of the regularly recurring crises. The only defence against the phenomenon continuing was the establishment of free unions. And here, with very great conciseness, he made the commission realize that, around that condition in the first point, a new value had arisen, the omission of which would upset the whole scheme. The government side realized, on hearing Wałęsa's calm but emphatic words, that they were facing a final and determined demand from the workers such as they had never before experienced.

After the meeting all the journalists wanted to speak to Wałęsa. It is obvious that he was pleased with the result of the talks, but he avoided any further comment apart from making some general remarks. In the hall there was bitterness and disappointment that the commission had such exiguous powers. Voices were raised saying that the praesidium was talking 'soft' and to accuse Lech of not pressing them enough: 'We should not have given them Coke when we only had water – they should have been made thirsty.' Wałęsa tried to defuse the nervous tension. He tried to lift their spirits. He threw out some slogans: 'We shall prevail', 'We won't give in', 'We'll endure'. Recent hopes have been dashed, and doggedness reappeared. When he sang the National Anthem one could feel that each word of that song was taken very personally by all those present.

Sunday, 24 August. In the morning Mass, confession, communion. Waiting for news from the Commission. In the afternoon nothing happens until the moment when, with some delay, the final fragments of an address by Edward Gierek in the plenary session of the Central Committee of the Party are relayed. They are received coolly, with remarks that this was 'tepid tea' and not an answer to the principal condition – the creation of free unions. When in the end Gierek asks the members of the Central Committee whether they have any questions or proposals, and after a while states 'I don't hear anything', there is an outburst of laughter in the Gdańsk hall. But when Gierek intones the Internationale, all present in Gdańsk get up from their seats and sing very loudly 'Poland has not perished yet' – the National Anthem. After the singing a forest of raised arms with clenched fists can be seen. Soon afterwards Wałęsa comes to the hall amidst enormous applause. Again clenched raised fists. Again the chant: 'Le-szek' 'Le-szek'. He jumps on the rostrum, takes the microphone and says a few simple words which in this atmosphere have a completely different meaning: 'Don't relax for one moment, not one step backwards. Only free unions, only those can satisfy us. We are waiting. We shall endure.' After a few moments he leaves the platform and again there is applause and the chanting of his name.

Wałęsa, sitting relaxed in an armchair, talks to a group of journalists. We ask what he thinks about the changes in the Political Bureau. He replies wittily that he has exchanged six and now is waiting for the rest. At that moment he realizes that he has said too much and asks us to cross out this sentence. Some journalists are recording him, others, like myself, are making notes. A friend of Wałęsa's snatches the notebook from me, wanting to see what I have written. There is a sharp altercation. We struggle. They threaten to expel me from the shipyard. At last Wałęsa intervenes and pacifies them. We revert to our conversation. Wałęsa informs us that the praesidium of the MKS were consulting with the experts on how to work out a formula for free unions. He admits that events have out-stripped his boldest expectations. He thought that the possibility of creating free unions would not arise for a year or two. This is why he needs expert advisers – he is unable to think it all out himself. 'I'm making a revolution in a situation when we only have the outlines of a programme. Of course, if socialism were strong, it would defend itself against destruction and against free unions. Szydlak's speech in Gdańsk doesn't interest me.* I'm doing my job. For the time being, I have a collection of disparate good things, but most of all I need free unions. On the Coast there will be a nucleus of a new force that will spread beyond this region. Almost everybody belongs to the present unions now, but what is wrong is that they didn't impose their own tempo. And yet the unions are the key to the solution of our problems. They must participate ... We also need the Church very much – it doesn't do any harm. It only instructs people. We must liquidate the censorship which is throttling us ... I feel very tired when I get into bed, but when something happens I revive at once.'

Ever more journalists approach, many of them foreign. They ask about his assessment of the situation again, about changes in the Political Bureau. This time he replies differently: 'I'm not interested in personal changes in the Party. We have our own programme for which we're fighting and from which we will not draw back.'

On Tuesday, 26 August, talks began at last. During a break in his meeting with the commission, Wałęsa tells the delegates: 'My position is clear – you know it – and unchanged, and we'll see what happens next.' In the second round of talks, Jagielski tries for the umpteenth time to push the discussion about trade unions towards the modification of the structure of the CRZZ (Central Council of Trade Unions). He keeps repeating that they are agreed that criticism of it is justified, that they are willing to reform the unions etc. To make matters clear, Wałęsa points out that they

* Jan Szydlak was a senior member of Edward Gierek's ruling group, and at the time was in charge of the official trade unions.

are not concerned with improvements, but want new unions. But even this does not help. A new diplomatic manoeuvre begins, interrupted by Wałęsa's short sentence: 'Will they be free or not?'

Later, Wałęsa remarks: 'I'm waiting for a negotiating partner who could settle this. For the moment I can't see one.' The sentence is immediately taken up by foreign journalists. A small crowd gathers round Wałęsa's armchair in the small hall. Flashlights explode, the journalists switch on their tape recorders. It is obvious that Wałęsa is very pleased with the day's talks. He develops his programme more and more. 'I don't seek further strikes in Poland. The force which I have got here will suffice. The strike mustn't spread becauase it paralyses life too much. If, however, we can't settle matters ourselves, we shall reach for that ultimate weapon. We need the threat of a strike, not its actual development.' To the question whether he thinks that it would be necessary to spread the strike beyond Poland's frontiers he replies: 'I'm now only interested in Polish affairs. Perhaps when I stand higher, I might be interested.'

About himself he adds: 'I don't care about anything. I shall settle the matter of free unions and that's that. I want only to be a worker. I don't wish – simply don't wish to study further in any schools. And will you repeat this' – turning to the lady translator – 'I haven't been to any other than a trade school. I'm doing everything for the cause. And I don't care about international renown, only about our cause.' He is pained by memories of December 1970: 'In 1970 I was also in the shipyard and remember those colleagues. I must ensure that their sacrifice results in the realization of their desires. Their monument will be in the shape of a cross. We shall stress by this that they were religious people.'

I can still remember well the moment, reported all over the world, of the signing of the agreement between the Government Commission and MKS that ended the eighteen-day strike at Gdańsk and relieved the tension throughout the country. I can recall Wałęsa's words about the necessity of bringing about agreement between Poles. A few minutes later, in the hall of the BHP he announced, amidst enthusiasm, a meeting for 16 December round the monument to the dead shipyard workers. The emotion which everybody then felt was accompanied by a feeling of relief and a release of tension.

One realized at that time that the understanding reached during the discussions was the first step in the process of change that the strike had instigated. It was quite natural that, having been with the shipyard delegates during the strike, I wanted to be with them when they were fleshing out their programme. This was not easy, because the sequences of events did not allow one to participate in everything. One had to choose. Not wishing to get confused by all that was happening, I made notes about everything. Later these might turn out to be either important information or small trifles. But the first days that made one realize that history was being made on such a scale that the whole country was interested, and that only by accumulating these trifles would one be able to understand much that was happening around us. It also allowed one to understand the personality of Wałęsa, as it was developing against this background.

It was an event unlike any other in the history of People's Poland.

I shall revert to my notes of 1 September 1980, which was the first day after the strike: Already several minutes before the formal transfer of the premises allotted for the union a group of people had gathered there, and the journalists and photographers were very active among them. On No. 13 Marchlewski Street, a white-and-red flag appeared with the handwritten inscription: 'Inter-works Founding Committee of the Free Trade Unions in Gdańsk'. At 10 am Lech Wałęsa, chairman of the MKZ,* held his first small press conference in the building. But he had no time to talk. He just invited the journalists to meet him in the evening. In fact, there was no possibility of any dialogue because former delegates or representatives of many factories and institutions, not only from the Three Towns but from all over the country, were arriving all the time. The premises, a flat put at the disposal of the independent union, were unsuitable for such a function. There was no room or space anywhere. Small groups formed, always around somebody from the praesidium of the MKZ. People asked for information, for explanations, for advice on how to act. A box was quickly found to serve as a container for written questions. At any given moment, somebody was pushing a note into it. After a short time there were hundreds of notes

* MKZ stands for the Polish words for Interworks Founding Committee.

– on application forms or on small scraps of paper torn from diaries. At midday some order was established among the crowd of people arriving. Some people stood in the doorway and directed others to the first organizational meeting.

At 4.15 pm the meeting with the factory delegates and those who wanted information about the new trade unions began. Of course, not everybody interested could find room in the premises of the MKZ, so the meeting was transferred to a Gdańsk secondary school. Its big hall was full and many people had to stand in corridors and outside, under the windows. Loudspeakers were set up to transmit the proceedings. Everybody was taking notes, because the organizers transformed this first meeting into a kind of instruction session on how to act when forming new unions in plants or workshops. The pile of questions received during the first day allowed the experts of MKZ to prepare some practical suggestions. Questions were also asked in the hall, and immediately answered by Wałęsa.

His answers were quick as lightning. He had many ideas of his own and rarely resorted to the help of his advisers or people from the praesidium of the MKZ. From his answers a certain common programme began slowly to emerge, in many places not entirely clear, but pointing the way: the implementation of the agreement, the question of wages and the place of the new unions within workplace structure.

Wałęsa explained that the enormous amount of work awaiting the new union could not be borne exclusively by the works' delegates or by the initiating committees. Gradually he made us aware that no one would do our job of creating something new for us. During a lively, at times mass-rally type, discussion the sentence which, slightly changed, was later to become a kind of slogan, was uttered: 'Our unions are new not in name only; what they'll be like, how they'll work and how they'll be organized – all that is up to us.'

In the first days of September, deputizing for Lech Bądkowski, I participated in the work of the praesidium of the Gdańsk MKZ for a few days. This was a completely new experience for me. I got to know people whom I had previously seen directing the strike but whom I now had the opportunity to observe in completely new roles as leaders of a growing union movement. It was

at this time, too, that the first and extremely acrimonious confrontation occurred between Wałęsa and Andrzej Gwiazda on the
subject of the principles by which the union would be directed.
That confrontation also marked the beginning of a constantly
recurring mutual antagonism which reached its climax in the open
letters to each other published at the beginning of April 1981 and
in the election campaign for the post of chairman of the Gdańsk
MKZ.

Later I also took part in meetings of the praesidium at which,
each day to begin with and then every so often, I used to prepare
a review of the daily and weekly press. It was then that I also
started to analyse more closely Wałęsa's effect on his surroundings,
both behind closed doors and at huge mass meetings. I often went
with him to those kinds of meetings. I accompanied him for whole
days at work. I took part in mass rallies and meetings, and I
listened to his conversations in the office.

I also met his family. I tried to maintain some distance, so that
I would be able to judge him dispassionately. This was not easy,
because his strong personality, with its typical leadership traits,
could not be easily defined.

Wałęsa, famous all over Poland since the strike for his actions
in Gdańsk at the beginning of September, also gained great
authority in the newly organized centres of Independent Self-
Governing Trade Unions (MKZ NSZZ). The inaugural meeting
of these unions was held in Gdańsk on 17 September. I will quote
here a fragment of my report written on the spot and later censored:
'At 4 pm members of the praesidium of the Gdańsk MKZ NSZZ
and their experts took their places at a long table. Behind them
on the wall were the national emblem and the cross that had hung
in the Gdańsk shipyard during the strike. There was tension in
the air. It was 4.10 pm when Lech Wałęsa rose and greeting all
the delegates said: "We must work effectively and act to satisfy
all of us. This is why we shall discuss all our complaints, all
problems, and what is to be done about them. We shall discuss
them as equals for the benefit of us all." He asked another member
of the praesidium, Lech Bądkowski, to take over as chairman.

'Looking at the crowded hall, I realized that it contained only
delegates, two from each local workshop and from large factories.
It is evident that they formed a large group. And yet this first

meeting of the MKZ was being held only seventeen days after the signature of the agreement. During this short time so many branches of the MKZ were formed in Poland that it was possible to call a first information meeting. People had flocked in from all over the country. They spoke in front of the microphone, and colleagues from other centres busily made notes and often recorded them. None of the speeches were specially written – they all came "from the heart": greetings for Gdańsk, for Wałęsa, for shipyard workers and also very concise statements of where and in what way the MKZ or MKR* had been formed, how many workplaces they served and how many registered members they had. The speakers did not omit their complaints and anxieties. They spoke fluently, informally, detachedly. No one exceeded the regulation five minutes. All spoke with contained passion.'

Slowly from these reports there emerged a picture of the new trade-union organization, not yet possessing approved statutes, not yet registered, but having three million members. This was a mass movement. Every few moments there was an appeal for unity: 'We shall conquer with unity,' 'Strength by unity,' 'Let's form a common front,' 'Our strength is unity.' Each speaker was applauded. Everybody awaited Gdańsk's reaction. The organizers pointed to the need for an elastic regional organization. It would be that organization which would give them strength. But no. This is not what they were after. They wanted to have a common body which would co-ordinate and lead the weaker centres. Wałęsa interrupted again and again. He said that the new unions did not want to repeat the mistakes of the old ones; he rejected the idea of creating a new central union organization. He pleaded and pointed to the weaknesses of the previous system. All in vain. At last he couldn't take it any longer. He became excited. 'Yes, this unity problem. A difficult thing. You may think that I made a mistake, although I don't think so. But I'll tell you that when I met the Venerable Primate Wyszyński, the Central Council of the Trade Unions arranged a plenary meeting and suggested that I should take the lead.† So I could have had that unity. I didn't agree. I don't want such unity.' (Applause, shouts, bravos.) 'This

---

* MKR stands for Inter-Factory Workers' Committee, a variant of MKZ.

† Cardinal Stefan Wyszyński (1901–81) was Primate of Poland from 1948 until his death. His influence over the population at large, and Wałęsa in particular, was profound.

is why they concluded – because there were some robust minds there – that if that didn't succeed one must try something else: that we should make sections, branches and other divisions, that we meet in Gdańsk and aim consequently at centralization. No. This is not the problem.' Now he began to speak slowly, stressing every word. 'We must create a Co-ordinating Commission, but we must complement one another so as not to lose the room to manoeuvre. This means that a vigorous centre, with strong MKZs, can help the weaker ones. Even by strikes, but not by instructions from the centre. No one should attempt, not even Gdańsk, to influence those MKZs centrally. Of course, on some matters we shall agree, but not as a commission. Because they would then transmit to their branch what we have been discussing, and the decision would be taken at the bottom. That decision would be binding, but not the instructions of the commission. This is the way we are planning our activities. So that unity should not be reached too fast.' (Applause.)

The atmosphere in the hall was becoming electric. These were no mere appeals but demands to create a common front: 'Gdańsk is strong and can now afford to be independent, but such a plan would be short-lived, because after the liquidation of the smaller centres the time would come, and quickly, for Gdańsk. Look how we are treated inside the country.' True: the picture was uniform and sometimes gloomy. In some workplaces, and also in towns, the authorities and management, wanting to satisfy the demands, helped in the creation of the NSZZ. They provided the union with premises, gave permission to use duplicating machines and even allowed the use of cars. In other cities, and even in central offices, there was a narrow interpretation of the agreement as applying only to the Coast. This created a number of conflicts and tensions, and even sometimes led to strikes in which the demand for permission to create the NSZZ was put at the top of the list. There were examples of small centres where people spoke about the new unions in whispers behind closed doors. This created a certain distrust of the local authorities which on the one hand agreed to independent unions but on the other hand did not agree that they should function in their area. Hence the appeals to Gdańsk, to Wałęsa, to the shipyard workers to take the small centres under their wing, and especially to take the initiative in creating branches. Those voices demanded a common front. This was also the stance of the Co-ordinating Commission, which proposed that all the already existing MKZ NSZZ should seek a common registration – as one union. This founder union would not have the right to interfere in regional matters or in basic organization in the factories. It was also agreed that one should clearly state the distinctness of the new unions from the old/new ones that arose from the breaking-up of the Central Workers Trade Unions, and therefore it was agreed that the union would adopt the name of Solidarity.

The proclamation of these decisions and the election of Lech Wałęsa as chairman of the Co-ordinating Committee of the new union was greeted by applause from all those present.

The final moments of the first meeting of the MKZ of all Poland brought a distinct relief among those present, who, in a more relaxed atmosphere, then tried to find out whether they could obtain help from 'the mighty' – especially from Gdańsk, because the city had became the central point of activity of the new trade unions. Somebody even threw out a jocular suggestion 'to accept the bondage of Gdańsk'. 'They thought out everything for the best, they have collected the best minds and they have Leszek Wałęsa.' They did not, however, want to avoid the independent creation of a new reality, but wanted only to exploit the experience and successes which Gdańsk had achieved, first the MKS and later the MKZ. For them the capital of Poland had become Gdańsk and not Warsaw.

The fifth hour of the meeting of MKZ was approaching when Wałęsa took the microphone and began to speak about himself. He seemed tired. When the applause stopped, he suggested that everyone should sing the National Anthem. He sang it first in his strong voice. The others joined in, including those who were listening outside the open windows of the Rowing Club. 'Poland has not perished yet' – these words acquired a special meaning now.

The outside world was becoming increasingly interested in the new movement and especially in Wałęsa himself. Starting with the 'Gdańsk summer', all the more serious journals, weeklies and illustrated magazines carried articles about him. Scores of articles and photographic reports were published, and there were many interviews. People talked to his wife, to his neighbours, to his comrades at work and in Solidarity. They wanted to know everything – about the years of his early manhood, his activities, his family . . . even his childhood. They also looked for sensational news items and sought the reasons for his popularity. People were writing about Wałęsa in all the main languages of the world. The first books began to appear even before articles on the Gdańsk strike. Those most interested in Wałęsa however were the Italians, the Japanese, the French, the Scandinavians, the Germans and the Americans.

Journalists who frequently visited Gdańsk realized how important in the union, and even outside it, were Wałęsa's views. In Western Europe, in the United States and in Asia, especially in Japan, people were fascinated by his personality. The new trade-union movement was assessed through his person. By tradition, at the turn of each year, the readers of many publications select their own Man of the Year. In 1980 this honorary title was awarded to the Pole, Lech Wałęsa, by readers in the German Federal Republic, Denmark and some other countries. And in countries where he 'lost', as a rule he came second to that other great Pole – Pope John Paul II.

Had such an opinion poll been conducted in Poland, he would without any doubt have been the only candidate for the title. His popularity within Poland is beyond belief; hardly a day passes without a number of delegations inviting him to visit their MKZ, factory, institution or even apartment. The organizers of the new trade-union movement, artistic circles, writers, students, agriculturists, vie with one another for his presence. He has to open festivals and officiate at great assemblies. He went to Lublin to greet the winner of the 1980 Nobel Prize for Literature, Czesław Miłosz, at a specially arranged meeting, and four days later he acted as host to Miłosz at the Gdańsk Lenin shipyard. He travelled all over the country. He 'extinguished fires', talked to people in clubs, conference halls, in the corridors of the institutions he visited, he talked to miners underground, to crowds in vast stadiums, to ministers, to the First Secretary of the Central Committee of the Party. He persuades, explains the principles of Solidarity, admonishes those who, in his opinion, fail to observe the union principle of common action, those who have been 'outmanoeuvred' or have been 'bureaucratized' or have forgotten that the party rank-and-file have to decide. He demands that the union should be democratic. For him democracy is not just an empty slogan but the real possibility of a common working-out of attitudes. He often said that one must learn democracy 'because, frankly speaking, I have had enough of the kind of democracy as practised in our union. Everybody thinks differently and in the end one must trust somebody, for if thirty-five million Poles all want to rule, we shall never reach agreement. One must elect somebody for this work, which in reality is a service. We have not so far learned to appoint suitable people.'

He was outgrowing the tight union 'uniform' in which some people would like to see him. He was becoming a union leader who formulates his programme not only for today but for the future. In these activities he was repeatedly forced to make decisions which may be defined as political. He was fighting all the time against the 'hotheads' in Solidarity and the 'toughs' among the authorities and the Party. Even in the most dramatic moments he did not let his emotions get the better of him, especially those that would incline him to change the moderate line of Solidarity. He then spoke about political patience. He spoke about it to the intellectuals, to the peasants and to those workers who, in his opinion, go on strike quite unnecessarily. On such occasions he was not afraid to face a crowd and berate it, nor did he hesitate to take a stand against its expectations. He also knew how to oppose his closest collaborators, not only in a small group but also at a public forum, disassociating himself from them quite distinctly and demanding that they accept his line of conduct. He then talked toughly about the need for realism. He realized that a single unwise step might jeopardize the whole process of reform. He repeated constantly that there was no need to invite anyone else to solve our problems and that it was not necessary to pay the highest price – in blood. One must, he maintained, seek solutions that allow one to get out of every impasse, but he did not favour compromise at any price. He knew full well that in the whole period of existence of People's Poland so many injustices were inflicted on our people that one fine day the nation would lose its patience and explode. He recognized such a possibility and therefore he tried to dissipate the growing social anger to prevent its exploding too violently. 'One must control this anger and contain it,' he says. 'I know how to do it because I know how to argue.'

He constantly repeated that he did not dabble in politics. During the strike he had unequivocally stated that politics do not interest him. He still repeated this, but in fact he must have begun to realize that more and more often, from sheer necessity, his actions involved politics, and not local but global ones. This involvement in politics, resulting from the difficulties of the process of reform in Poland, the shallowness of our political life, was forced upon him. He did not seek it. He wanted to be merely a trade-unionist, but the situation in Poland forced him to act in a way which his adversaries always defined as political. Asked if he ever wanted to be a politician, he did not deny that an improbable situation might arise in which Solidarity would have to take over the government – although he believed this unlikely. If responsibility for governing the country should fall on Solidarity, he would then be the first to accept that responsibility. And although he considered that this would be a fantastic, extremely improbable situation he believed that he would be able to steer the ship of state.

Many people who have heard or read such statements by Wałęsa consider them to be purely theoretical or even ludicrous. Personally I don't reject them. Moreover, I consider that the internal situation in Poland might precipitate Wałęsa's emerging as the man of the ultimate hope.

Wałęsa represents a new type of trade-unionist, not only for Poland but also for the world in general. A trade-unionist who wants to serve the people not only in Poland but all over the world. But he puts the national interest above that of the trade unions. At one of the meetings he declared bluntly: 'We are not here for great politics, but to serve the people.' Frequently he is able to speak sharply not only about others who have not justified the hopes placed on them, but also about himself – that he has been so engrossed in his work as a 'fire extinguisher', as an arbiter and as a kind of last hope for all disappointed people that he has distanced himself too widely from the workers. Yet their strength is his strength. He wants to be their spokesman all the time. He always seeks contacts. He throws himself into a confusion of meetings, despite the fact that he has been subject to incredible stress since the August strike. He is desperately tired, his health is not too robust and his heart is strained. He feels that what he achieved in August was his greatest success and one that he won't ever be able to repeat. He was happy when he was signing an agreement with the Government Commission, because he realized that this had come about in the nick of time. People would not have waited much longer, doubts would have arisen and a reaction might have set in that could have undermined the whole of the August achievements. He considers however that the supreme moment of his life has not yet come; nor the worst. He is unable to be more precise about one or the other: he feels intuitively that time works to his disadvantage. He is a fighting man. He realizes this and yet aims to achieve social peace. He foresees however a time when the economic crisis will deepen, the queues at the shops lengthen, and his popularity decline. And the same people who so recently applauded him and carried him shoulder-high will begin to stone him and trample on him, forgetting that he was acting for their good. He knows that he can then quit, shave off his moustache, and return to his beloved shipyard, but he does not want to do this, because he thinks that his feeling for a given situation can be useful at critical moments. On the other hand he cannot retreat, he must go forward all the time. Without him the movement would lose its wide social resonance. Society would lose its symbol of hope. This symbol allots him a role that he has assumed not because he was just doing a job, but because it was necessary for the good of the country, to strengthen its independence and democratization. He has come to identify himself with Poland and he is proud to be Polish.

It took only a short time for this unknown electrician from Gdańsk to become the unquestioned workers' leader, enjoying great authority among the working people of the world and among politicians. It was Helmut Schmidt who used the expression 'the Wałęsa phenomenon', and politicians, through their trade-unionists, solicit visits from him, especially at the approach of presidential or parliamentary elections. During the last presidential campaign in the United States it was anyone's guess which of the two parties would be the first to obtain the prize of at least a reflection of Wałęsa: as it turned out they got Lech's stepfather, Stanisław Wałęsa, who has lived in the United States from 1973. Similarly, Valéry Giscard d'Estaing's party wanted to exploit Wałęsa's planned visit to France in March 1981. The sudden cancellation of that visit thwarted their plans. It was said that Giscard, strongly attacked by the Left, especially the socialists and French citizens of Polish origin, for his 'friendly contacts' with Gierek and for his lack of interest in the fight of the Gdańsk workers in August 1980, had lost much of his previous authority, and Wałęsa was to have helped him to gain votes in the presidential election. The same thing happened in Japan, preparing for the 1982 parliamentary elections, and in Italy, when the competing trade unions wanted at least to improve their image by playing host to an untarnished trade-union leader.

Wałęsa's personality shines very brightly outside Poland. I accompanied him on his two trips abroad and I must say that his behaviour impressed me greatly. When he went to Italy, it was his first foreign journey. He entered a world in which the media play an enormous role: they can quickly turn someone into a television or press star, but they can equally unmask a shallow person at once. One can say that the meeting of Wałęsa with 'abroad' occurred in the view of the whole world, because the Italian and Vatican meetings were held in the presence of representatives of television and the press from all over the world. Even in the plane on the way to Rome, journalists tried to interview Wałęsa, and television and film cameramen tried to catch some characteristic details of his behaviour. When his plane landed the media had a field day. To cover the reception, the Italians alone sent cameramen and reporters from three state television channels. The programmes were transmitted in Italy and then relayed all over the world.

The welcome that took place recalled the storming of a citadel (Wałęsa) by a crowd of journalists and other representatives of the media. They came from American stations NBC, CBC and ABC, France's RFN (two programmes), the BBC (with representatives also of the Polish Section), from Mexico, Brazil, Austria, Belgium, Holland and Greece. There was a group of special representatives of press and radio, numbering about 150 people from Europe, both Americas and Japan. Apparently this was the largest gathering of journalists and television and radio people ever to attend anybody's arrival.

Before Wałęsa came the newspapers speculated on the nature of this first foreign trip by the Polish trade-union leader. The headlines questioned: 'A pilgrimage or a trade-unionist's visit?' But already at the airport Wałęsa dispelled all doubts by saying that he came to Italy to meet the Polish Pope and that he came to him 'like a son to his father'.

As the plane touched down the interest in Wałęsa reached its zenith, but the excitement lasted for the whole period of Solidarity's visit, from 13 to 19 January 1981. As I wrote at the time:

'Each step of the delegation was recorded by television cameras, hundreds of photographers, reporters and representatives of colour magazines, the main radio stations and the world's biggest news agencies. It was not only very wearing, but one gained the impression that journalists were brutally seeking for sensational tit-bits. Some attempts were made to promote Wałęsa to the rank of a minor film star. One felt that Western journalists wanted to find a new idol symbolizing popular protest and the lightning political career of a single man. They were fascinated by the Wałęsa phenomenon. Yet Wałęsa and the delegation behaved with coolness and sobriety, thwarting all attempts to create a myth. They also rejected suggestions that they might have something to report about the internal situation of the country. In spite of inevitable "nerves", the members of the delegation were not to be persuaded to make any statements about Polish politics. Wałęsa shocked some people by his persistent claim that the main object of his visit to Rome was a pilgrimage to the Holy Father, not a trade-union meeting. Only after he had visited Pope John Paul II did he relent and give several interviews to the press, radio and television. The first television interview, for Italian television, occurred immediately after his visit to the Pope, while he was still at the Vatican. The last one was for one of the Catholic television stations, Antenna 4, directed by Father Vergilio Rotondi, a Jesuit and the founder of the religious movement Oasis, which also exists in Poland. The interview was published in *Il Tempo* a week after Wałęsa's departure from Italy. Between these two interviews there were scores of others, short and long.

'Everybody in some way prepared to exploit the charismatic personality of Wałęsa, a star against his will, for his own objectives. As *Le Soir* wrote (on 15 January 1981), his presence in Rome "might have been cynically exploited by the Christian Democrats for showing the defeat of communism, and by the communists for stating that it is possible to combine a one-party government with the principle of pluralism". The publicity that accompanied his visit caused everybody to wait impatiently for the main press conference expected on the fifth day of the delegation's sojourn in Italy. It was to have been a "political sensation". The press were looking forward to checking up on Wałęsa, but after the meeting all commentators agreed that he had demonstrated great talent as a "people's champion", calmly answering even the most difficult questions and proving that he will not be provoked into making any political pronouncements that might undermine his fidelity to the Polish *raison d'état*.

'The other conferences were of a similar nature. It is perhaps worth mentioning the one which, on the first day of the delegation's stay, was to have been a kind of test. It was to have been presented by French television, but French viewers were disappointed on that day, because the interview with Wałęsa, planned even before he left Gdańsk and already announced, did not take place. Wałęsa's decision was a shock for television journalists, who just could not conceive that a man about whom the whole world is writing and talking should refuse to participate in a programme to be watched by several million people, for the sole reason that he treated his journey to Italy as a pilgrimage to see the Pope. They had never yet experienced such a situation. The delayed interview took place after his audience with the Pope. Relayed "live", it showed the French the way of thinking of a man already famous in their country. *Le Monde* wrote of that conversation that it was "the art of avoiding questions, especially those that concerned his private life and the state of his country's economy". They quoted Wałęsa as saying: "Of course you live better than we do, you possess more things, but are you happier?" In turn the communist newspaper *L'Humanité* mentioned the disappointment of those interviewers who expected to be able to transform the meeting into a "judgement on Poland". Wałęsa's calm contrasted with the excitement of both the French journalists, and the contrast was heightened by Wałęsa's apposite responses in which he managed to accuse the French of not being fully informed about Poland and the views of Solidarity, which is "in favour of socialism".'

During that interview, just as in front of the cameras of Italian television and at other meetings, Wałęsa was exposed to many loaded questions intended to provoke him into making statements of a political character. He invariably answered them calmly, rejecting all attempts to give the press conferences or conversations the character of political debates. During his public appearances he did not shun – indeed one could almost say that he seemed to invite – questions concerning the differences between the activities of Italian and Polish trade unions. Constantly stressing the common struggle of the working people all over the world, he pointed out the differences in the social and political systems of the two countries and the resulting necessity for each to work out its own, specific methods of operating.

After the first interviews, and especially after the main press conference on 17 January 1981, the *Frankfurter Rundschau* defined Wałęsa as an 'ideal subject for a press interview', taking the opportunity to add that he had 'a distinct charismatic charm, trenchancy of expression, clarity in formulation and a pleasant wit'. His improvised speeches and his jokes showed the Italian working people that here was someone like themselves, and they did not fail to respond in a typically enthusiastic manner.

The most important moments during the visit were the two meetings with Pope John Paul II. For those meetings, one can say without exaggeration, the whole world was waiting. One realized that the origin of these was John Paul's pilgrimage to Poland when, under the eyes of the whole world, he lifted the hearts of a whole nation.

When he went to the Vatican Wałęsa surprised his closest advisers, who, aware of the importance of the meeting with the Pope, had asked him to prepare his speech. He rejected all suggestions of the kind because, after his experience of reading from a sheet of paper at the end of the strike and at the un-veiling of the monument to the dead shipyard workers of 1970, he knew that his talent was for unscripted talks, and he decided to speak to John Paul II in that way. To be sure, as he mentioned later, at one moment he was afraid that he would lose the thread and would embarrass the Pope, but he quickly recovered himself. So he spoke 'from the heart', though he was nevertheless able to outline all Solidarity's most essential objectives.

The photograph of that meeting showing Wałęsa kneeling in

front of the Pope, who is about to lift him to his feet, was distributed all over the world, and the picture's symbolism, expressing the homage paid not only for himself but on behalf of his nation, was emphasized. To describe the atmosphere of this unprecedented meeting, I can quote a French journalist, Robert Serrou: 'You see here facing one another two giants, two men, two legends, two Poles who in a miraculous way appeared in the glare of history. These two who until recently were virtually unknown brighten – we don't know why, or perhaps we know all too well why – our Earth as it stands on the verge of despair. They appeared in the East, heroic but poor – their only weapon their strong faith, both struggling against the folly and threat of all the enemies of Man. Unmoved, inflexible, like romantic knights of the old legends, fighters in a peaceful crusade aiming only at gathering the support of all people of good will against the assault of barbarity. They make you smile, because they fight with their bare hands, yet with such conviction that their confidence seems unshakable. Here is the modest metal worker from Gdańsk, applauded today as a real King of Poland, Lech Wałęsa, and the former actor from Krakow, elected Pope in 1978, the only unquestioned leader of the twentieth century, Karel Wojtyła, who became John Paul II ... Wojtyła – Wałęsa – engaged in the same contest. They both know it. Just as they know that their meeting has real historical meaning: each of them in their way is the personification of hope, not only for the countries of Eastern Europe, enclosed in their dehumanized communist ghetto, but also for the whole West, paralysed by fear and resignation, more preoccupied to satisfy its selfish needs and its own safety than to listen to the powerful summons of love in the souls of every individual. The summons that cannot remain without an echo, that at the sight of the smallest spark of hope is ready to renew itself ... Here are these two men, and how exceptional they are! ... What luck for mankind, what luck for every man. How fortunate that their meeting has come to pass' (*Paris Match*, 23 January 1981).

There were similar comments from the main press agencies. The Italian papers representing the Centre, the moderate Right, the Left of all shades, socialists, social democrats, liberals, communists and Christian democrats, wrote the same. They pointed out that more journalists came to the audience than came in October 1978 to the Vatican when the Conclave was taking place.

A similar interest was taken in Wałęsa when he went to Japan (10 to 16 May 1981). It lasted from the moment of his landing at Narita airport near Tokyo until the delegation returned home. As in Italy, Wałęsa was personality number one in Japan. One must stress, however, that his difficult and exhausting star role suited him down to the ground. He was able to adapt himself to every circumstance and situation: he was amusing and jocular when he spoke to schoolgirls, serious during his meeting with parliamentarians, relaxed with trade-unionists and with students. In every situation he was himself: he did not pretend to be an intellectual, and he always stressed his working-class origin. Yet he behaved as a man who knows his worth. Listening to the more experienced Japanese trade-unionists, he did not fail to point out that they had lost their courageous spirit, becoming more like functionaries than activists. He reminded them that the strength of trade-unionists was in unity of action. What he saw in Japan seemed to him like a denial of the experiences of the working class so far: there are deep divisions between many trade unions and the resulting lack of a common platform of action reflects negatively on the situation of working people.

Moved by the size of the human tragedy at Nagasaki, he spoke in talks with journalists about the need for action towards the creation of international solidarity. 'Men have prepared such fate for men. It was not done by workers or peasants but those who had led their country badly. Today we can draw conclusions from it, but is this lesson enough? And if it is, those who saw it should remember and shout aloud. No matter who they are, they should from time to time stop and think what heritage they would be leaving. Of course, machines and watches are pursuing us. There is no time for thought, but one ought to stop for a moment. We Poles have a Christian faith, so it is our duty to stop at least once a week and look back at what we shall leave behind us. I represent trade unions, I am not a politician, nor a member of the government, but it is the world of working men which I represent that must force those who are responsible for us to remember. I should not like to see ever again such monuments. We must not allow this.'

The Japanese received Wałęsa and the whole delegation with enthusiasm. For the second time that year they experienced the fascination of the Polish character, for in February John Paul II had come to Japan on a pilgrimage of peace. Wałęsa brought closer to them the human dimension of Christianity and the specific role of the Catholic Church in the history of the Polish nation.

It was also remarked that Japan has been host to three important representatives of Catholicism. First came the Pope, then in April Mother Teresa from Calcutta, the Nobel Prize winner who appealed for charity for the starving and the sick, and now Wałęsa joined them with his appeal for human dignity and social justice. This lightning advance of the unknown electrician from Gdańsk to the position of moral leader of workers all over the world could turn the heads of most men. Some people claim, it is true, that this adulation has made him conceited, but I think that he has simply matured, begun to be more thoughtful, begun to diverge from the set pattern of his earlier pronouncements, realizing even more the need for order in every person's soul. Only such a person is capable of realizing great schemes.

Legends are now circulating about Wałęsa and his whole family. They are kept alive by sensational bits of information. The most frequent is the piece of gossip, repeated for many months now with various modifications, that not all the children are his. Once somebody asked him directly at one of the first meetings of the Gdańsk committee of the MKS: 'Are all the children yours?' On reading that question passed up to him on a piece of paper, he looked puzzled, but with typical relaxed jocularity he answered: 'I've never thought about it. My wife always tells me that they are mine. I've no reason not to trust her.'

In conversations and at meetings he always speaks warmly about his wife: 'A splendid woman, a good wife and an ideal mother. It's she who supports all of us, although it's hardest for her. She's more of a hero than I am.' He realizes that his own contact with his six children, aged from twelve years to ten months, is almost non-existent. The eldest, as he often says, has followed in his father's footsteps, and is wild at school. With the others, there are also problems. His wife has to see to everything. For about ten years he was periodically arrested and there were other tensions. Just before the strike, he was arrested and detained for distributing leaflets protesting against the imprisonment of two of his comrades. This was the time when his youngest girl was born. Children are his joy. Like any other loving father he worries about not having time to take them for walks, to check their homework, to play with the youngest two girls, 'my princesses', to be at home when a child is crying or when it is sick ...

Immediately after the strike, the Wałęsas were allotted a new flat. It was found for them at once. Before that they had lived for many years in two rooms with an area of twenty-odd square metres. One night, after the strike, the offices of a housing co-operative were vacated and three standard flats, M-2, M-3 and M-4, allotted to them. One flat was made out of these: six small rooms, two small kitchens and two bathrooms. Some people cannot forgive them for having such a flat. After their move, Wałęsa's wife Danuta went to the neighbouring block to have her hair done. While she was there she learned from one of the two customers present that 'a fellow has moved in who visited the Primate – Radio Free Europe broadcast it – a man who had lived in luxurious conditions and yet now they have given him a whole floor. One cannot imagine how luxuriously appointed it is. A new form of communism is beginning. Why do they have so many flats for themselves?'

Danuta could not stand it any longer and told the woman who she was. The woman then became confused and, not knowing what to do, began to justify herself: 'It's not me who's talking like this, but other people are.' Others have said that they hoped to bribe Wałęsa with the flat, to soften him up. It is a fact, however, that at the very beginning of September it was suggested to Wałęsa that he should move to Warsaw, where he was to take over the leadership of the Central Council of Trade Unions (CRZZ). They promised him the earth, displayed before him the mirage of a beautiful furnished villa and other facilities for his family. He rejected all that and said he wanted to receive only what was due to him. During the full assembly of the Gdańsk MKZ he asked me if he should accept the bigger flat offered to him. He was advised to take it, so he moved in.

Numerous invitations from many central trade-union organizations, such as the Italian, Japanese, French, Danish, Swedish, West German, and US, as well as from the Committee of Defence of

Human Rights, prove his popularity throughout the world. He has received various prizes. The most recent of these was the prize of the Swedish Social-Democratic journal *Arbetet* awarded for his activities for the workers' movement. The prize was called 'Let Us Live' and amounted to 50,000 Swedish Kroner. After receiving it in Malmö Wałęsa turned over the money to his union. And not so long ago, as he tells with amusement, he, a simple worker, received the title of Doctor Honoris Causa from one of the Cambridge colleges. He also holds the title of 'First Pipe Smoker', as well as many other honorary distinctions. At the beginning of February last, the press of the whole world suggested the names of candidates for the Nobel Peace Prize 1981. The three candidates put forward by the Norwegian parliament in Oslo were: the Prime Minister of Zimbabwe, Robert Mugabe, the former US president, Jimmy Carter, and the leader of the Polish trade-union movement, Lech Wałęsa.

Another sign of his popularity are the letters he gets. Adults and children write to him. He receives several letters and postcards every day. It is characteristic that the majority of Christmas wishes are accompanied by a Christmas wafer. He is constantly asked for his autograph. People write telling him about their day-to-day personal worries and about the most serious matters affecting the country.

His wife also receives very pleasant and friendly letters. They are addressed variously. The post has delivered letters to 'Lech Wałęsa, Solidarity, Varsavia'; 'Prime Minister and Wałęsa – Poland' (this one reached Gdańsk); 'Lech Wałęsa, Gdańsk, Poland, Europe'; and 'Lech Wałęsa, spokesman for the Catholics in Poland'. Once a letter arrived from a teenage Polish boy with the request that he should write to his father who was cross with him because he liked Wałęsa.

There are people not content with writing: they request personal interviews. Although Wałęsa sets aside two hours daily for seeing visitors, this is not enough. They come from all over Poland and from abroad. Sometimes they wait for several days to reach his presence. There are also cranks with inventions or revelations. None of them want to see anyone but Wałęsa.

People from abroad mostly come to interview him for the press or collect material for books they are preparing about the problems of contemporary Poland. They talk to many people, such as representatives of the Church and of the government, and finally, as if to sum up, there is always an interview with Wałęsa.

People come under any pretext to see him, exchange a few sentences, perhaps take some souvenir photographs and obtain his autograph. Even his flat is not free from callers. His very pleasant and pretty wife complains that people sometimes ring their bell even at night. She dare not open the door because it always transpires that the caller wants to discuss something urgently and immediately. The board on the door saying that this is the Wałęsas' home and that callers are received at his office does not help. Once a woman with a small child arrived at night. She came because she was sacked from work and had no one to help her. She took her child and got the next train to Gdańsk. She found the address at once: it was enough to ask at the station for it. She was directed to Zaspa, a new district of Gdańsk. There, everybody, in every shop and every kiosk, knew where the Wałęsas lived. The family is constantly in the public eye; some people even tell taxi-drivers to take them to see their block of flats; others stop under their windows and stare. The Wałęsas have got used to it, but they have been accosted by unknown people, even in church, and made to listen to whispered confidences. Drunks have knocked on the door to complain about family quarrels, as have wives molested by drunken husbands. They don't want to complain to the police, they prefer to see Wałęsa. All this shows the trust he enjoys. It results from the myth that he is able to solve all problems.

He himself is permanently in a hurry. He says this is unavoidable. He does not know how long he can stand the pressure. He wants to be ready and prepared for all situations. He does not spare himself. He is troubled by ill-health but has no time for treatment. He swallows pills, and carries on as before. He is chasing the passing time, as if he wanted to catch up with the wasted years. He is on edge when he has nothing to do or when no callers are waiting, and wanders around the rooms of his apartment.

He takes on his shoulders such a burden of work that he cannot cope with it. He struggles with problems, all at the same time, each more important than the last. Every decision is important. He makes mistakes, but is not afraid to admit them. In the first months after the strike his days began very early and ended often as late as 10 pm. Now it seems that he is working at a more leisurely pace, yet the tension is greater than ever. He is more mature now when it come to taking decisions that affect the whole country. He is not afraid to take ones that can cause protest or even the resignation of some of his nearest collaborators. His working day still begins very early, for, if he is at home, he goes daily to Mass at 7.30 am. A short Mass and communion. 'This is a good beginning for the day,' he has said. 'Later, I never know what may happen.' He returns home, swallows his breakfast and at nine begins work. Sometimes he rushes home for a quick lunch and then goes back to the office. He is constantly on the move, with no possibility of taking a rest. Although his collaborators try to protect him from the callers always waiting in front of his office and to persuade him to stretch out for a moment in the afternoon or even take a short nap on the camp bed, this doesn't help much because then he would have even more people to see later.

Wałęsa likes talking to journalists. He frequently finds a moment to answer them quickly and concisely. Serious purpose mingles with humorous sallies, malice with humour, demagogy with intuition. He gives many interviews; in the view of the Gdańsk praesidium of the MKZ and KKP,* too many. In spite of the remonstrations of his staff he does not limit them, he likes them. With a popularity like his, it is difficult to avoid them. He even grants interviews to people who are known to be critical of Solidarity and of himself. He never edits and 'authorizes' the text of an interview. He leaves that to his staff, whereas previously he left the interpretation of his thought and intentions to the readers. They, he believes, are capable of separating falsehood from truth. The journalist's duty is only to pass on his thoughts: 'If he is honest, he will try to report on the usefulness of our work, and if he is unfriendly, we would have difficulty talking with him anyway.'

In conversation, it is best to attack him. Under attack he comes alive and talks brilliantly. I have seen him many times, since the strike, talking to visitors. I have also observed him talking in Italy and Japan. He has two ways of approach. When speaking to foreign

*KKP: Polish initials for National Co-ordinating Committee, Solidarity's provisional executive until the union's first congress in the autumn of 1981.

journalists he sometimes condenses so much that it is difficult to follow the train of his thoughts. But if the same question in the same conversation is asked by Poles, he tries to explain himself in more detail.

He does not like looking at the past. This he leaves to history – it will judge what was good and what bad: 'The past is for historians,' he says now, but during the strike, and also in the first months thereafter, he felt the burden of it. He looked back at December and its lessons. He would revert to it: 'This was my biggest mistake. If I had been the man I am now the chances in December were that we would have achieved what we have got now. But I was then twenty-seven and knew very little. I didn't have any experience. But during these last ten years I've analysed and thought back over every detail. The bloodshed obliged me to do so.' Now he says: 'Don't let's look backwards, but forward. This past is in all of us, the real work is before us.'

He realizes the strength of the union. More than once he has thrown all his authority on to the scales in order to reduce the tensions that began to build up between Solidarity and the authorities. He extends his hand in friendship first, although often this does not have any effect on his adversary. He persuades the members of the unions to work for consolidation in workshops, warns them against provocations inside the union, and also against attacks on our allies, especially against anti-Soviet provocation. He speaks about this at meetings during his journeys round the country, at meetings with the NKZ, in press and television interviews. He knows that he is under attack both by the radicals in the union and by various forces in the country who would give a lot to stop the dynamic rise of Solidarity.

Wałęsa stresses the need to re-value the objectives of the union, which, after a period of consolidating its authority and of confrontation, must pass on to the stage of carrying out the terms of concluded agreements. These must be sorted out because quite frequently they are mutually exclusive or duplicate one another. More attention must be paid to the rank-and-file. They have somehow become lost in the fight and in confrontation, and in decisions being taken by the leading activists, and not on the shop floor. Agreeing with the opinion of many that it is the authorities who must present the necessary complicated plans for improving the state of the country, he believes that one cannot wait indefinitely for this to happen. He is still unable to develop this idea fully and illustrates it with rather naïve examples. He listens to what others have to say and suggests that this is a subject for the experts, who should try to develop his thoughts. He listens to the experts, but takes decisions himself.

He says: 'I am an ordinary worm on this earth. Don't provide me with glory.' He wants to be treated as an equal by others. He wants to remain himself: the same man as he was before the strike. Does he succeed? Hardly. Things have changed too much. He himself has changed. Externally: he no longer wears a loose coat and trousers let out at the waist and for official meetings he dons an elegant suit and wears a tie, although he dislikes ties. He is weary of observing manners, listening to advice and instructions. In an interview with Oriana Fallaci he said about himself: 'I'm strangled by a tie and why should I smile when I don't want to, when it doesn't please me? And I'm not allowed to do anything now. I can't take a drink or lay hands on a girl, as if that would be the end of the world. They say that I've become conceited. This is unjust. You must admit that it is unjust, for people remain the same even if they are in politics. Everyone is a sinner and commits little trespasses' (*Corriere della Sera*, 7 March 1981). 'At work,' he says, 'I feel best in a sweater, a denim jacket and corduroy trousers.' His hair has been cut shorter lately, and his moustache trimmed.

Wałęsa is a very religious man. During one interview, a journalist from *Le Point* kept stubbornly reverting to this fact. At a certain moment he asked Wałęsa whether he had wanted to become a priest when he was young. Wałęsa answered, laughing: 'Before, I didn't want to, now I might, but it's too late anyway.' He has some of the traits of a preacher who tries to convince people but leaves the final choice to them. He himself made his own choice: at first he was a believer because this was expected; later, between his seventeenth and nineteenth year he distanced himself from his faith. He threw himself into wild living: dancing, parties, girls, drink. 'And then something happened: one day I had a cold, was very tired and I looked for a place to sit down. And as there was no such place nearby except a church, I entered the church. I sat there on a bench – it was warm – and at once I felt so well that I've quite changed since. No, I'm not an angel. I'm more a devil. But I go to church every morning, I receive communion every morning, and if I have a bigger sin on my conscience, I go to confession. I do it, because after all I'm a decent man – I don't have many sins to be absolved from. In all my life in this world I have been drunk twice – once when I was in the army and the second time when I was in a trade school, because of a girl' (Oriana Fallaci's interview with Wałęsa).

Wałęsa's religiosity has no intellectual content. It is simple, sincere and strong. In faith he has found an additional 'something'. That 'something' was developed in him and he has felt a need to deepen his attitude to religion. This process was speeded up by the great events in which he has actively participated. In religious meditation he always finds hope. So it was during the Gdańsk August, when the tension and the expectation of the use of force seemed to break some people; Wałęsa at such moments would sit down somewhere apart and detach himself from these problems even if only for a moment. 'I commended myself to the Virgin Mary. I commended to Her our destinies. This gave me courage and strength.'

During the strike, daily public prayers, confessions and communions and Sunday Masses confirmed and strengthened his faith. In one of the first interviews after the strike, Wałęsa said: 'I myself believe. I derive strength from faith, it's the motor of my life. I've always given public expression to it, but if anybody thinks differently, I don't interfere. But during the strike, many people, under those specific conditions, under permanent psychological stress, reminded themselves of the basic moral and ethical values with which they had been brought up. And that morality is sustained by the Church, which also spreads the truth. We lacked that truth at the time. Thus we sought it in God's word as proclaimed by the Church' (WTK, 5 October 1980). Another time he added: 'Many people understood then that what the Church has been saying for two thousand years is the same thing as we are fighting for.'

He reaffirmed this belief every day of the strike when he prayed, received communion and sang hymns; when, a rosary round his neck and using a fountain pen bearing a photograph of the Pope, he signed the agreement that ended the strike and began a new stage in our lives. His first act in the newly opened union head-quarters was to hang up a cross he brought from the hall where the striking delegates had held their debates, and to place there two pictures from No. 2 Gate of the shipyard. He understood, however, that in union offices one cannot make little chapels or altars because not only religious people belong to the union. Hence in his office the historic cross and rosary and a photograph of his visit to Primate Wyszyński hung for only a short time. Later the cross was transferred to the conference hall in the now famous Rowing Club where it was mounted on a beautiful piece of coloured canvas in a frame next to the national emblem; the rosary and the photograph are at Wałęsa's home. Questioned frequently by journalists about the influence of the Church on Solidarity he has always replied that these are two separate matters: 'Sometimes we walk together, sometimes we walk apart. Occasionally one must go against what the Church advises.'

The Church for him is not only a place where faith is cultivated, but also an institution that has never left the Polish nation to its fate. In his pronouncements Wałęsa often pays tribute to the now deceased Primate of Poland, Stefan Wyszyński. It was Wyszyński who revealed to him the complexities and problems of our political life. It was also through the good offices of the Primate that the Pope invited Wałęsa to visit him in the Vatican. Wałęsa is fascinated by these two great Poles and he speaks of the late Primate as having been a man of immense wisdom, whom he trusted absolutely. He considered him the man of the greatest moral and political authority in Poland. He accepted his comments and suggestions because they were always well thought out and always looked to the future. The Primate has helped Wałęsa when the latter could not cope with the peasants or the workers. His authority sustained Wałęsa. Solidarity also owes a lot to him.

Wałęsa often speaks of his faith: 'If I was not a believer, I would not be the man I am. Faith is necessary in difficult situations, but later people abandon it, as we did, in Poland, because life with faith is not comfortable and because there are great tempta-tions. But if you are not a believer, it would take too long to explain it to you. You must take my word for it. Faith is indispensable' (interview with *Le Monde*, 21 March 1981). In another interview he said: 'Faith is something very private for me. My relaxation.

When I sigh a little, I don't fear heart failure. Perhaps it is like yoga for other people. Religion is my peace. Therefore my strength ... If it were not for faith, I would have let you down a hundred times' (*Tygodnik Powszechny*, 25/26 December 1980).

In Italy at a press conference he said: 'Our faith has not hindered us in anything, but rather helped us to perform our human duties. Our faith is an individual means of expression for every human being. No one interferes in these personal matters. It is a very personal thing for every human being. It is of importance for me, but it is my personal affair ... If I am here and speak to you it is because during the twelve years when I have fought for the unions and had many hard days, I sustained myself by my faith, and I am here now. If I had been unbelieving, I certainly would not be here. I believe that every man has faith in something – one perhaps in money, another in his career, still another in ministerial office – and therefore I can endure everything.'

After the strike, all the three plants (the Gdańsk shipyard, ZREMB and Electromontage) where Wałęsa had worked since 1967, and from which he was in turn fired, expressed the wish to reinstate him. He is now formally employed in the Gdańsk Lenin shipyard in section M-4, as an electrician, delegated to work in the NSZZ Solidarnosc.

June 1981

Chapter 4

The Man of What?

Lech Bądkowski

The alterations and additions to the constitution of the Polish People's Republic introduced under conditions of inexplicable haste at the turn of the year 1975/6 were greeted with some reservations and even opposition in Polish intellectual circles, especially in creative circles. They produced collective protests, especially from Warsaw. Not having the opportunity to join any of the protests, I decided to write my own paper. In February 1976 I passed it on to the president of the Provincial Committee of the Front for National Unity at Gdańsk, considering that under the existing formal structure this was the proper political address for me. I gave copies of it to the press and a number of people occupying institutional positions in public life. I also distributed copies privately.

I did not receive any official answer, but news about the existence of my paper somehow spread locally and aroused interest in student circles. Thus on a spring day in that year two young men called on me and asked if they could have a talk with me. One of them was Bogdan Borusewicz, of whom I had already heard.

From then on I began to interest myself in a small group of local people having their own views about the realities of our situation. It consisted of persons unknown outside their narrow milieu, in which the principal, almost the exclusive, part was played by young people.

In June 1976 came the memorable increases in the price of foodstuffs that provoked immediate protests by workers, especially in Radom and Ursus. These were followed by police and quasi-judicial repressions (judges who pass political sentences in a country with an authoritarian regime can only be considered as quasi-judges). In September of that year the Committee for the Defence of the Workers (KOR) was formed. Soon afterwards, Boruszewicz became one of its members.

On 29 or 30 April 1978, the Founding Committee of the Free Trade Union of the Coast (KZWZZW) was formed. This was a group initiating an authentic workers' movement concerned with the living standards and social rights of the working class. It was an attempt to give body, amongst the working class, to the demands voiced by KOR. Lech Wałęsa belonged to that group and this was the first time that I heard his name, which was still not widely known. I did not meet him in person at the time.

As far as I know, while participating in the Founding Committee of the WZZW and signing its declarations, he remained as it were on the fringes of the committee. He belonged to it but went his own way, and probably was an ally rather than a real member. I must add however that at that time I knew personally only Borusewicz from among the founders. I had not even heard of Anna Walentynowicz.

I came into contact with a larger group of independent young people at the end of June 1978 in connection with the appeal of Błażej Wyszkowski, the brother of Krzystof Wyszkowski. They were both active in the creation and work of the committee (KOR). At that time I also came to know another independent group, the Movement of Young Poland, which arose from the Movement for the Defence of Human and Civil Rights or, more precisely, seceded from under Leszek Moczulski's wing.* The other young people involved who had just finished their studies or were still studying were Alexander Hall, Arkadiusz Rybicki, Dariusz Kobzdej, Magda Modzelewska and Leszek Jankowski.

Contacts and meetings became more frequent. A very strange situation arose in which there were thunderous propaganda assurances about the brilliant and astonishing developments in Poland, about prosperity and great achievements, and yet ever more widely,

* Leszek Moczutski was a maverick figure in the various opposition groups of the seventies. At first associated with KOR, his views were more conservative and nationalist than those of men like Jacek Kuroń, and he eventually became the leader of the extreme nationalist group known as the Confederation for an Independent Poland (KPN).

although still only in some social circles, an independent movement
of protest was developing. But I still had no contact with Wałęsa.
I did not know him or hear any more about him.

In March 1980 successive so-called elections to the Sejm (the
Polish parliament) were held. Because of this the Founding Committee of the WZZW and the editorial offices of *Coastal Worker*
(a subsidiary of *The Worker*, published by KOR) issued a pamphlet
calling for a break with the ritual of passive voting for one list of
candidates and advocating either the crossing-out of the names of
the candidates or non-participation in the voting. As I considered
the election a fiction, I did not vote. The pamphlet was signed by
eight people: Bogdan Borusewicz, Andrzej Bulc, Joanna Duda-
Gwiazda, Andrzej Gwiazda, Alina Pieńkowska, Maryla Plońska,
Anna Walentynowicz and Lech Wałęsa.

Then came the Third of May. The anniversary of the historic
constitution,* the first written constitution in Poland and in Europe,
previously pushed into oblivion, had been brought to the attention
of the people of Gdańsk, and to a certain degree to the people of
Poland, a year earlier, at the instigation of the Movement of Young
Poland. The celebration of it was repeated in that year, 1980. While
distributing leaflets printed to mark the occasion, Wałęsa was
arrested and held for forty-eight hours, as were many other people.
During the demonstrations on 3 May by the memorial to King
Sobieski, two speakers, Dariusz Kobzdej and Tadeusz Szczudłowski, were sentenced to three months' imprisonment by the lower
court. Both appealed and in July the court of the Second (last)
Instance at Gdańsk considered the case. The formalities were
preserved: the higher court did not confirm the sentence.

While Kobzdej and Szczudłowski were under arrest they went
on hunger strike for a time and were forcibly fed. There were
prayers on their behalf in the church of the Holy Virgin Mary. Lech
Wałęsa participated in the service. On that July day when, after
the service, the participants were standing together in a group in
front of the church, Alex Hall pointed out Wałęsa to me. I was
quite interested to see him, but not to the extent of wanting to meet
him.

* On 3 May 1791, the Sejm passed a new constitution inspired by the principles of the
Enlightenment and the French Revolution. Under the postwar communist règime, the
anniversaries ceased to be celebrated.

From all this it emerges that in my estimation Wałęsa did not appear to be a VIP. I heard of him as a deeply committed man, outstanding for his versatility in the still smallish group of activists of the free unions, but not a real leader. I don't believe that anybody considered him as such at the time, which may explain why I had not heard any opinions that might make me look at him with more interest. I was, however, at that time almost exclusively interested in the theoretical and ideological problems of the democratic movement in Poland and also in the political possibilities of its influencing certain sectors of power to refrain from indulging in repression. I did not therefore devote much time to organizational activities, apart from distributing uncensored publications and participating in discussion meetings. Hence my knowledge of the activities of the Founding Committee of the WZZW was sparse and from that circle I still knew only Borusewicz and Krzystof Wyszkowski.

(Here a note is necessary: it is not easy to establish a reliable list of founder members and any list is open to interpretation, because in this case, and no doubt in many others, the degree of engagement of people varied and the act of founding the organization had not yet been legalized by the setting-up of a proper office. Secondly, there were often quarrels amongst the founders, and resignations and even vendettas were frequent. I was told for instance that Krzystof Wyszkowski had been expelled. I also heard, as I have already mentioned, that Wałęsa should be included among the first founders of the committee. Lastly it is well known that, while defeat is an orphan, success always has many fathers, very often jealous of one another. After the event more than one person will be ready to claim a father's role that was not his, while denying credit to those who deserve it. This, however, is another question. Also involved in the process of the creation of the committee and later Solidarity, as is always the case in movements arising spontaneously, were certain combative, anarchic people, in principle negatively disposed to the existing order.)

From the beginning of July 1980, the time of introduction of a new, clumsily concealed rise in the prices of foodstuffs (the introduction of 'commercial prices'), there began a time of social unrest in Poland. Strikes broke out in many towns, and these resulted in an increase in wages, though limited to the striking workforce alone. On 14 August a sit-in strike started at the Gdańsk Lenin shipyard. It was followed by similar action by the workers in other large plants, a general strike in the Three Cities and afterwards in a wider area of Pomerania. A spontaneously organized workers' committee of self-government did however exclude from the strike those branches of production and those services that were essential for the continuation of a more or less normal life, such as railway transport, health services and power stations.

At the very start of the strike in the shipyard, I heard Wałęsa's name, but only in a general context, although he himself, out of work at the time but a former worker at the Gdańsk shipyard, found himself among the active organizers of the strike on 14 August and next day became the head of the strike committee, quickly rising to lead it and exert increasing influence within it. The fact that I had still not met him might have been the result of the activities of the media, which provided only misinformation at that particular time. In the television news programmes on 14 August, for example, there was a short item about 'cessation of work' in the Gdańsk shipyard and nothing more. In my 'Notes of the Day' of 15 August, in an entry before midnight, I wrote: 'As I understand it, Lech Wałęsa has risen to be the head of the strike committee. Also active in it Anna Walentynowicz'. So something percolated through to me all the same.

On 17 August in the late afternoon I found myself for the first time inside the Gdańsk shipyard, together with Stanisław Załuski. It was a Sunday, and a decisive day, as it appeared later, for the continuation of the strike. Yet even then I did not have an opportunity to talk to Wałęsa, because he went to bed tired by his previous efforts. I did, however, meet Anna Walentynowicz. From my conversations at the shipyard it became clear beyond any doubt that Wałęsa had become a personality of prime importance.

On 21 August, after several days of preparation, a meeting took place of all those Gdańsk writers whom one could notify and assemble. A proposed statement was presented and its text finally agreed. About 3 pm we found ourselves, in a fairly numerous group of members of the Union of Polish Writers and its Youth Circle, in the shipyard in a building called BHP (because it had been used for lectures about safety and hygiene at work – Bezpieczeństwo i Hygiena Pracy in Polish), inside a large hall where the plenum of the Interworks Strike Committee was in session. Before we got there from the gate, where our credentials were checked and the purpose of our visit explained, news of our arrival had reached the hall. Wałęsa, standing on the platform surrounded by the members of the praesidium, announced to the delegates that the writers had come to tell them something important and invited us to the platform. He added, only to me, something like: 'Well, at last our literary men are here.' Afterwards, when our statement had been read and received with enthusiasm, Wałęsa embraced me.

Thus I met face to face a leader who within the next few days was to become one of the best-known Poles in Poland and in the rest of the world.

I have reported in detail what happened before that day of 21 August because I want to stress two things. First, the difficulties and slowness in the process of meeting people of kindred interests when they are active in unfavourable conditions, without the normal means of exchanging views, trapped in artificial social structures. Second, that Lech Wałęsa, in the four weeks from the middle of August to the middle of September 1980, in spite of being accepted as the leading figure in the trade-union movement in Poland, remained completely unknown, except to a small group of worker-colleagues in industry and to activists connected with the Founder Committee of the Free Trade Union of the Coast.

Today I know considerably more about the WZZW of before 21 August 1980, but only from documents and conversations held afterwards. In this article I shall, though, describe the state of my knowledge about these matters, and about Wałęsa in particular, at that period.

An understanding of the two facts mentioned above shows the enormous problems that were facing Poland in this period of internal reform. Thirty-six years after the end of the Second World War, after a lengthy period of building our Third Republic, we have been forced to thrust forward to exceptionally responsible posts people about whom we knew very little because we ourselves have had no opportunity to meet them and there was no time for them to prove their worth by their actions. I am not speaking about Wałęsa alone, but about all the activists in Solidarity and the other organizations that started to spring up or revive after a long-lasting sleep. A strike, like any act of protest, may be a very significant gauge of character, but it is one-sided and does not testify to the leader's mental capabilities and skill in other areas. This only refers to people who have come to the fore after the August events.

Such a situation, seemingly absurd after thirty-six years of a state's existence, applies also to the Communist Party, because when its leadership suffered a sudden thinning of its ranks at various levels, the names of the alternative team could not signify anything to society at large. This is the price that has to be paid for lack of democratic methods in public life.

Now I wish to consider what kind of man and what kind of a leader I consider Lech Wałęsa to be after nine months of acquaintance and close observation.

First of all he talks a lot, willingly – indeed rather too willingly – granting interviews. The quantity of his statements that I know of – and I'm sure that I don't know them all – not only creates the impression of excessive volubility but could also lead to false judgements. I feel that he is not always as sincere and as easily decipherable as he would like to appear. This statement is not necessarily derogatory. Whether he likes it or not, as the head of the trade-union movement he is, and must be, a political personality, especially in a country of such peculiar constitution and in such a delicate position as Poland.

Wałęsa's loquacity may perhaps be an effective offensive method of screening the undoubted shortcomings of his leadership. What strikes one most is his readiness to reply at once during negotiations and verbal arguments. Frequently his ripostes are good and accurate, sometimes even excellent, but quite often they are only a manoeuvre to mask the lack of an answer or even lack of knowledge of the subject.

Wałęsa does not like to show that he does not know, that he would like to think about something, or at least seek somebody's advice about it.

This trait is coupled with physical mobility. He walks fast, gesticulates freely, talks easily. He is humorous and likes making jokes – about himself as well, though this does not mean that he likes being criticized. In personal relations he tries to be amiable and polite, in spite of some roughness in his disposition. So far he does not strike attitudes – in personal relations of course – although he does not listen attentively to what people say to him if it is not what he wishes to hear. But on the whole, he is sure of himself and a trifle conceited.

He must always have had qualities of leadership, otherwise he would not have joined an independent movement and would not have come to the fore in a striking Gdańsk shipyard, especially when he had not worked there for some years. His advancement was due to a favourable set of circumstances, especially his election to be chairman of the Interworks Strike Committee (MKS), encompassing the Gdańsk area and some other plants scattered around Poland. The striking workers and the whole protesting community wanted unification and were looking for a leader. All eyes were turned towards Gdańsk, especially to the Lenin shipyard, because it was there that the events of December 1970 began, where the protest started effectively, although it was then bloodily put down. The expectation that Gdańsk would 'do something', because it had already done it once, was irrational but none the less universal. A favourable situation was thus created and Wałęsa immediately appeared. Did he realize the far-reaching consequences of such a turn of events? A moot question, for who could foresee the events at all? All we know is that he filled the gap and came out on top.

At first no one seriously considered a concrete programme for the movement and its projection into the future, because the movement was only the protest of a mass of working people. The list of twenty-one demands, speedily compiled, seemed enough. Everything that arose in each new and quickly changing situation was an improvisation that succeeded by an extraordinary amount of luck. One such unplanned, and very propitious, factor was the spontaneous help of intellectual circles. It is to Wałęsa's credit that he immediately appreciated the value of that help and accepted it.

Wałęsa thus stepped without hesitation into the leading role without having the organization necessary for such an enormous undertaking and without, as I believe, fully understanding its real size and effects. Here it was his courage that came to the fore, the courage that often must verge on risk-taking, from which people of a more placid disposition would shrink in fear.

This courage is coupled with a capacity for leadership. Wałęsa has this in his blood: it is a folk leadership. He faces a crowd and speaks with ease as if he were addressing a few bosom friends. This at once made him into some kind of a people's champion. Standing next to him, I have witnessed a few such interventions. His listeners reacted spontaneously, with great enthusiasm. In his words there was nothing extraordinary, nothing that could by rights inspire the people, no revelation or call to act. I listened and observed unmoved, because these speeches repeated all the well-known slogans and phrases, with little asides appealing to popular taste, almost in the style of a stand-up comic, and yet people lapped up every word, every gesture, and responded with glee, rapture, admiration. This was undoubtedly because he talked simply, in their own language, speaking as any one of them might, only just that little bit better – because, after years of cant and turgid speech, they were hearing ordinary everyday talk, mistakes and all. This was however a revelation for them, something unusual, because the speaker was a simple leader of their own choosing and from their own part of the community.

But it is not only this that has brought him such enormous success. Many more leaders spoke to them, and they listened readily and applauded. But Wałęsa has a gift known as charisma. Everybody admits this. It is difficult to define this innate gift of the gods, although it has been known for centuries and has been analysed by sociologists and, earlier, by theologians. Only a few individuals have it, and they come from very different circles of influence. In this respect Wałęsa has gained the Polish championship, the first since Piłsudski or ... Gomułka. Today only a few people remember how great was Gomułka's popularity in October 1956, what a charismatic figure he cut. Yet the charm dispersed very fast.

Charisma cannot be acquired, but one can instinctively or skilfully build on to it and increase its effect. This is what Wałęsa has done in publicly demonstrating his religiosity. This brought excellent results when contrasted with the official laicism (and semi-official atheism) of the authorities who were being undermined. Field Masses, religious songs, holy pictures, rosaries, introduced an atmosphere of exaltation under conditions of threat.

One must at once add a rider: charisma in sociological terms is a dangerous attribute. It is based on qualities appreciated and supported by society, but the qualities of a person recognized as being charismatic can be real or only apparent. It can also appear as the mixture of the two. It cannot be measured by objective criteria, only in retrospect. One cannot therefore deny that Wałęsa's enormous success was to a considerable degree based, and is still based, on a sham, an illusion, wishful thinking. So one does not know how he might behave in a moment of truth.

At the end of March 1981, the weekly *Czas* published an interview with me by Tadeusz Bolduen entitled 'The Hunger for Moral Leadership'. The interview took place in the middle of January, but that is only a bibliographical detail. Bolduen said:

'I am convinced that Lech Wałęsa is not a leader who measures up to the times or the tasks facing Solidarity.'

To which I replied:

'Lech Wałęsa is a figure historically accidental – an example of how history can play tricks. The dilemma is that it was the hunger for moral leadership in Poland that caused Wałęsa's incredible elevation. And in such a case one must not try to sober people down because one would then deprive them of something they have achieved with great difficulty and accepted with great joy. And yet one knows that this man, although he is a symbol of a breakthrough, is not the expected leader. The leap from being a persecuted unemployed man to being created Man of the Year in the West, to the covers of illustrated magazines sold in millions of copies, to a personality giving interviews to the press agencies of the world, to magazines and newspapers, could only be made by a man with great inner culture, an incorruptible man.'

That fragment caused a small explosion among the activists of Solidarity; perhaps it was a smokescreen for the anger that the next reply to the question 'And what about others?' caused:

'There are no others of a suitable intellectual level, which is nothing unusual, because how could leaders arise in that environment?'

I must stress something that escaped people's attention: that I spoke about an accident of history. Wałęsa did not prepare himself for his role. He did not climb the rungs of the ladder to leadership in stages, over many years, educating himself, improving his knowledge of politics and its key problems, and also of world politics. In our most recent history we find only one outstanding self-taught politician, Wincenty Witos,* but he made his way up

* See note on p. 140.

the social and political hierarchy only gradually, under the eyes of ever widening circles of the community. I assume that Wałęsa did not dream of the role he came to assume, although today he might speak or even believe differently.

Wałęsa's emergence was caused by accident, by fate, history, Providence, or, if one prefers, necessity. I continue to claim that the hunger for moral leadership made him into 'the little corporal' in Polish society from the second half of 1980 until ... We don't know until when. (I should explain here that it was the adoring old campaigners who nicknamed Napoleon Bonaparte their 'little corporal'.) I don't want to indulge in any guesses, but I must remark that the 'unbelievable elevation' of Wałęsa obliges him to make further efforts that only a genius could fulfil.

I have not yet mentioned all the circumstances that coincided. In August 1980 not only Poland's eyes were fixed on Gdańsk. The world that remembered December 1970 looked towards it as well. And there was more: Gdańsk in 1939 and Gdańsk in 1980 – this juxtaposition.as a possibility and a fear incessantly stirred world opinion through all the media. A Gdańsk on strike or rather the Gdańsk shipyard acted quite differently from the striking Szczecin or its shipyard (the seat of the Inter-Plant Workers' Committee). In Szczecin they shut the gate, cutting themselves off from journalists, with the exception of the local ones. Gdańsk was besieged by a crowd of reporters, first foreign, then Polish, and they were immediately accepted.

The presence of the world press assured great publicity to the Gdańsk strike and accordingly to Wałęsa. I don't say whether it was a good thing or a bad thing: I am merely stating a fact. Wałęsa became a world figure from one day to the next.

What I have written above is based to some degree on documents (mostly private), on some impressions, on personal feelings. I want to point out that, from the first meeting face to face, I was positively impressed by Wałęsa and felt good-will towards him. I was not seeking any moral leadership – this is a large concept and it is difficult to imagine its sudden advent – or political advice, but I was looking for strength and organizational skill within a programme of action.

Let's put on one side the programme of action. I must say that my observations lead me to think that Wałęsa has no organizational sense or even any understanding of the need for an orderly and productive organization. He is an improviser. A desk diary and its hourly divisions are entirely foreign to him. He talks to ten people at random, wastes time on unnecessary chores, and yet is frequently many hours late for important conferences at a high level.

There is chaos at the MKS. The callers know this. At first, one forgave him everything because everybody understood that things cannot be otherwise for a time. But months have passed and people wanting to discuss their affairs are being fobbed off, frequently because of sheer incompetence; more and more of them are disappointed and curse him. Wałęsa does not attach any importance to his own surroundings and their appearance proves it. One asks oneself whether this is only a continuing lack of understanding of how a competent organization should function, or whether it is also a feeling of his own importance and a kind of contempt for daily affairs as being of little importance. De Gaulle dealt personally only with great politics and he defined other problems, especially economic ones, with the word 'Commissariat', which sounded dismissive, almost contemptuous, in the mouth of a general/president. Wałęsa has probably never heard of De Gaulle's aversion for things he considered too earthy, but he has adopted a similar stance.

On 15 September 1980, two weeks after the setting up of Solidarity, I wrote a letter to Wałęsa. I considered that the definition of my attitude in writing, setting out several points which can be easily read and considered, would bring a better result than a conversation without such preparation. I believe that I am justified in quoting here the letter in its entirety.

Dear Colleague and Chairman,

We have collaborated for quite a long time, under conditions in which our acquaintance grew fast, so that I consider it as necessary and urgent to set down in writing these few observations for your attention and, if you think it useful, for the attention of the members of your praesidium and any other persons engaged in our activities or well disposed towards them.

(1) It is without any doubt high time to streamline and rationalize the system of work of the praesidium. We husband our strength in a chaotic and ineffectual manner. The number of meetings must

be reduced gradually and they must be limited in time. Besides one should:

(a) at the beginning of each meeting indicate clearly who presides over it and to whom all those present are subordinated in the formal sense;

(b) establish in advance the order of proceedings (under headings) and keep to this order leaving a small reserve of time for any other matters in 'free suggestions' as the last point of the agenda;

(c) keep an iron control on the speakers in the order established beforehand;

(d) discourage the introduction of other subjects and also loquacity.

(2) In the meetings of the praesidium only the following can participate:

(a) its members;

(b) experts invited by the praesidium;

(c) guests invited by name.

A meeting of a praesidium is not an open meeting in which everybody can take part.

(3) The meetings of the praesidium should be minuted. If we cannot afford that, there must at least be a book setting out what people have undertaken to do and decisions taken.

(4) One must urgently put order into financial affairs, produce a preliminary framework for a budget and spend money accordingly, obtaining each time a resolution of the praesidium for major expenditure. Otherwise we can find ourselves in trouble, and also be criticized by public opinion. I believe that this provisional budget up to 31 December 1980 should be published.

(5) One should aim at a reorganization of the praesidium in the near future in order to improve work and stress the areas of everyone's responsibility. This important task might be delayed, however, if a secretary of the praesidium (from among the members) and an office manager, responsible for the functioning of the administration, are not appointed now; one might also add a caretaker for the premises, responsible for its furnishings, cleanliness etc., both, I suggest, hired on contract. They must be very efficient people.

(6) The problem of the political position of our MKS is very difficult, delicate and fraught with danger. The text of the agreement of 31 August 1980 establishes that the unions associated with us 'have no intention of assuming the role of a political party'. It is obvious to me that, while not playing a political role, they would be a factor in social and political life, an important factor to boot. This makes our situation in the sphere of general politics in our country, and in the international arena, somewhat complicated. The importance of this came sharply to the fore during the strike, is apparent now and will be apparent also in the future. The real touchstone is the degree of interest of the foreign press.

I believe that one should not, only three days after the signing of the agreement and without discussing the matter, have invited as an adviser on to the MKS's praesidium Mr Jacek Kuron, a man undoubtedly worthy, but also controversial and with a very strong political bias. It is a good thing that, as far as I know, this idea has now been shelved.

All political problems that will face us, and there will be an ever increasing number of them, must be carefully thought over before any collective decisions are taken.

(7) The eyes of all Poland are directed on the MKZ at Gdańsk. People expect inspiration, advice, example and support from here. A symbolic and touching proof of this was the accession to the Gdańsk MKZ of the independent and self-governing trade union of the employees of the National Museum in Warsaw.

The current situation, for which we were not prepared and which was totally unexpected, puts an enormous responsibility on our shoulders. We must be equal to it – the situation and the responsibility – with honour and glory, or we will find ourselves in the pages of history as a group of noble amateurs who could not appreciate the enormity of its importance and lost it quickly, thus rounding off a most beautiful episode but one with very short-lived results. One way or another, history won't pass us over in silence.

The consciousness of these alternatives must be always present in our minds and must direct all our actions.

With cordial greetings

The points concerning organization and finance are very obvious. Perhaps it might seem strange that I should write out all these rudimentary demands, but they illustrate the initial situation. Improvement followed very slowly and within a limited area, mostly on the initiative of Wałęsa's collaborators in the praesidium. He himself read the letter at the time (he did it during a meeting at which I was present, so I know), put it in his pocket and did not react at all. Later, I tried several times to have a general talk with him, but without success. On the other hand he did not want to accept my resignation from membership of the praesidium. I explain this to myself as a wish on his part to keep in reserve somebody who might be useful also, or perhaps primarily, in personal matters.

Another example illustrates how difficult it was to foresee Wałęsa's behaviour while engaging oneself in his support. For reasons that are not known to me and which I did not attempt to discover, the supporters of Jacek Kuron in the praesidium of the Gdańsk MKZ decided to make a *coup d'état* directed against Wałęsa, or at least to force him to accept their political supremacy. At a meeting of the praesidium on 25 October 1980 five workers at the Gdańsk shipyard – members of Solidarity – were brought in. They asked to be given the right to vote, that is, in effect, to be immediately co-opted to the praesidium. It was against the rules, because only the plenum of the MKZ delegates could give such a mandate, and that was done because of the chaos reigning within the organization. Wałęsa sharply opposed their demand, arguing rightly that the next time he too might bring another five persons of his choice and demand that they also be given the right to vote. When, in an animated discussion, I took Wałęsa's side and used the words 'it would be a *coup d'état*', Bogdan Borusewicz, the would-be leader of the Gdańsk Kuron faction (also introduced to the praesidium by Wałęsa, although much earlier), became very angry but, clearly, could not advance any valid arguments. In spite of this, with all the other members of the faction, he persisted in his absurd claims. Wałęsa, seeing that the majority of those present might pass the motion, or at least abstain from voting, declared that he would suspend the meeting and leave it. Those who were 'for him', he said, must accompany him. There he made a mistake: from about twenty people present, only three left: myself and two others.

Later a fourth man joined us, a vacillating man who would have liked to have been able to support both sides and who left the praesidium soon after.

The die was cast, or so it seemed at least. We went to Wałęsa's room for a talk. I expressed the view that one must report the breach to the plenum of the Gdańsk MKZ and cause a revocation of the praesidium and the election of a new one. Wałęsa said that he thought so too. I asked if he had suitable candidates for a new one. He confirmed that he had.

We then prepared a programme for a meeting of the Co-ordinating Commission which was to be called for 27 October, and this became a matter of urgency, the more so because all this was happening during the period of frantic attempts to register Solidarity in spite of the government's attitude. And what could be done about the situation in the Gdańsk praesidium, when should one call the plenary session of the MKZ to authorize the changes? Wałęsa decided that, as a test, one must call a second meeting of the praesidium for the evening of the same day. He asked me to notify the members.

At 6 pm this second meeting began. All through it one might have thought that nothing at all had happened in the early afternoon. No one whispered one word about the bitter conflict and how to resolve it. It was rather peculiar behaviour for grown-up people. To those three who at the critical moment had voted for him, Wałęsa did not explain anything. He probably did not even think that he had a moral duty to do so. Only much later, when I reminded him of the incident directly, adding that by such behaviour he would estrange people who were loyal and friendly to him, did he begin to explain with typical animation and imprecision that at the time, between the first and second meeting, 'they' came to him and 'on bended knees begged him' to forget all about the incident.

I assume that Wałęsa simply was not sure that he would win his point, or perhaps did not as yet have enough trusted candidates for a new praesidium, and lastly did not understand the urgent need for putting order into the work of the leadership, whose members are not supposed to behave like rebels or children. One can give many examples of Wałęsa's lack of consistency, of his carelessness and lack of preparation. I am not, however, writing a chronicle of the beginnings of Solidarity; I am only quoting some episodes which show Wałęsa in a little-known light.

In my estimation, Wałęsa has many serious shortcomings. Perhaps he might try to improve himself if he realized clearly what they are and accepted, for a start, that they are real. This would not be easy because he has a high opinion of himself, he likes boasting and ascribes to himself all successes (including the extinction of the petrol fire at Karlino), leaving the setbacks to others.* He is jealous of his first place and shows it constantly, thus antagonizing other activists. He is compliant and accommodating only with the clergy. This is a separate problem, very complex and delicate, with which I cannot deal here. I will say, however, that some benefits have been derived from that attitude, although his excessive compliance has drawn criticism from his collaborators, of whom the majority are believing Catholics, but more objective ones than Wałęsa.

To sum up – I see Wałęsa as a man of instinct, not intellect. He is in my opinion a man of considerable innate intelligence that he has never tried to develop or refine. Previously, his circumstances made this difficult for him. Now he has no time or wish to do anything about it; perhaps he does not see the need for it. Moreover, he cannot husband his time so as to leave some of it to ponder on his own nature. He has also consciously accepted the role of people's champion who knows everything and is capable of everything and should be accepted uncritically. Thus the instinct with which he has been richly endowed dominates his intellect.

It is thanks to his instinct that he makes such excellent ripostes during polemical encounters. Thanks to it, he has been able to take harsh decisions and gain respect for himself as an adversary or as a friend. A very notable example of this capacity was that he averted a very great social and political conflict that arose after the events at Bydgoszcz on 19 March 1981 when a general strike had been called for 31 March, and a warning strike had already taken place on 27 March. The agreement between Wałęsa and Rakowski of 30 March averted the danger at the last moment. Wałęsa showed then

*On 9 December 1981, oil prospectors struck a pocket of oil and gas near Karlino, between Gdańsk and Szczecin, which ignited. It was many weeks before the gusher was extinguished.

that he had a sense of responsibility. He took risks with regard to the leadership of Solidarity because he exceeded his brief, and he was sharply criticized for it by the Co-ordinating Commission.

Perhaps one should call him a fighting man, for in a fight instant reflex actions, and the wish to shine and to succeed, play an enormous part. I should say more: he likes a fight, especially at its most effervescent. He is much less impressive in the daily rough and tumble, in a fight from entrenched positions that demands stubborn effort day after day and precise and intelligent organization, but no glamour.

During the first half of May 1981, at one of the meetings, I spoke about the problems of Solidarity and also about Wałęsa, not omitting some of his shortcomings. I met with criticism of 'stirring the Polish devil's brew', a reference to a then current joke.

This claim that Poles apparently like belittling those who have come up in the world in Poland I consider as exaggerated. Other countries and nations have similar faults; and often what seems to be a virtue in certain circumstances proves to be a drawback, and vice versa. When we compare ourselves to the Germans, Russians, French, British etc. we must remember that we have been living under difficult conditions as a nation for several hundred years, and also had very difficult experiences in the last few decades of our national history. This has created somewhat pathological phenomena like for instance the malicious gossip that surrounds Wałęsa and his family.

Yet I have not indulged in gossip. I have written of facts in good, although subjective, faith. Wałęsa is a new man; he appeared in public life suddenly and overnight in a leading national role, without any preparation for playing this role. If anyone wants to ignore the need for preparation he should ignore it; if anyone wants to believe in miracles he may do so; it will be a manifestation of 'voluntarism', an expression that has come very much to the fore during the last year. Apart from scientists, no one understands it, but as it is invariably applied to past rulers, everybody ascribes to it a pejorative meaning like 'licence', 'disregard for the law', 'despotism'. Leaving aside semantic reflections, one must state that 'voluntarism' is a much deeper and more complex notion. In the social sciences it means the belief in the rule of human will over the laws of nature and society, the absolutism of the subjective factor. It is quite a good footbridge to the cult of personality – which we already know about.*

Wałęsa is doubtless 'a personality' and creates the impression of a strong man. He makes this impression, but it does not mean necessarily that he really is a strong man. In front of him are many pitfalls, some of which cannot be overcome by instinct alone or a facility for arguing with other people. Wałęsa enthusiasts should remember that by putting him on a national pedestal, where there can be no criticism, by having absolute trust in him, awaiting a miracle from him, they cut off his feet. They take from him only what corresponds to their image of him.

Wałęsa once imprudently said 'we will make a second Japan'. He did not support this swashbuckling claim, but neither did he take it back, explain it or illustrate it with facts or figures. So we may do so. Let our people now work as hard, live as modestly, and behave in as disciplined a manner as the Japanese do. For many long years. But who really believes this could happen and who is there to put it into practice? The phrase slipped out of him; it was effective but devoid of meaning because another Japan cannot be created without the Japanese.

Taking into account all that I have said, adding to it the complicated conditions of the realities of the present in Poland, weighing it all up, observing the movement of the balancing scales, I will express the view that from among the leaders of Solidarity known to me, Lech Wałęsa is the most outstanding and, in a drastic condensation, the best man. At particularly critical moments he has shown responsibility for the fortunes of the country. He was no doubt reminded of this responsibility from outside and this is mainly to the credit of the former Primate of Poland, Cardinal Wyszyński. But in the last resort Wałęsa himself has to understand what he has taken upon himself.

The Wałęsa phenomenon will in future be discussed at length and in great detail.

The most important thing is undoubtedly Solidarity, the great social movement in Poland, descending to the roots of the nation and expanding into all spheres of national life. The force and effectiveness of that movement depend on all of us, together, on

---

* 'The cult of personality' is the official euphemism for Stalin's dictatorship.

the whole community, and not on a few individuals, however outstanding. They depend on our capacity to put ideals into practice,
on our strength to persist in a sensible stubbornness. This most
important matter will be our task for a great many years.

May 1981

Chapter 5

On the Difference between a 'Worker' and a 'Representative of the Working Class'

Maria Janion

I have never seen him 'live'. The first time I saw him was on television at the signing of the Gdańsk agreement on 31 August 1980, then in photographs and on film, and later again on television. How did he break through these barriers, through the seemingly inviolable fortresses of the small screen? How did he abolish the tested methods of creating official personalities? How did a live person get through to other live people with hardly any of those fake words and gestures which discredit the wholeness of a vital personality and are just echoes bounced off the impenetrable walls of propaganda? His image on television or in photographs was often set against the background of a crowd, which gave him that special, striking glow of life and blotted out the dummy men representing officialdom – or sometimes changed even them into real people. He would say – which instantly drew one's ears and attention to him – 'Speaking for myself ...' or 'Speaking for myself as a worker ...' The secret of his staggering success began to reveal itself: it was above all the secret of his speech as the expression of his person and the expression of a community. He imprinted his stamp as someone who was saying exactly what he wanted to say. And nothing more.

This praise of Lech Wałęsa's speech may seem somewhat odd. But I have a feeling that his way of speaking contained everything that led to his triumph. That he was able to be himself – a worker, a Pole, a Christian. That is the best way to define the steps of his progress, from the particularism of a life in a job to a more universal level of culture. At a time when bureaucratic irresponsibility and anonymity, with its subservient inhuman new-speak, a monstrous propaganda jargon, reached its final, absurd culmination, Wałęsa emerged from the crowd as an authentic man, free, angry, decisive, behaving directly and speaking plainly. One could hear amazed passers-by in the streets of Warsaw saying: 'What, an ordinary worker, and he can speak like that!' Probably we all, or most of us, were capable of talking like that ... But what was needed was a national arousal, an encouragement.

Wałęsa is aware of a hiatus between words and their sense, between what is said and what is thought and done. By the same token he guards against the terrible plague of official lies which has corroded and annihilated so much of social life in Poland. He stresses this by switching over to the third person: what Lech says and what Lech does is the same thing. Is he a lone man who has declared war on the television-and-press empire and won it? I would not say that. He had behind him all those who supported him by saying and doing the same as he. They gave him their support when by his tenacious action he had won their trust for himself – as a living person. The workers recognized their own features in him, but as if strengthened, magnified by magic. Because Wałęsa has grown to a national myth – a hero of the people. And that status is not, for the moment, inconsistent with his human nature. It may be because he is, it seems to me, a feeling, mediumistic person. To put it somewhat facetiously, not without significance here may be the fact that he is, by profession and calling, an electrician, that he senses currents and can master forces.

He behaves and talks as someone charged, electrified by the collective body. He is sensitive in such a way that he takes in that sensitivity and emanates it. 'I do not know if I am a leader,' he confessed to Oriana Fallaci, 'but when the crowd is silent, I know what it would like to say, and I say it.' He finds the right words, he knows how to 'control the most sacred anger of the people'. On 20 June 1981 Wałęsa was shown in television news countering a characteristically provoking question: 'They say you can do anything. Is it true?' So they talk about him like a fairy-tale mythical hero. Even if that question was a trick meant to make him compromise himself (after all, one hears sometimes that Wałęsa has a tendency to exaggerated individualism, and even megalomania), it turned out to be an opportunity for him to define himself in a very significant way. He denied that he could do anything. But at the same time he seemed to confirm it. How did he present that omnipotence of his?

Well, he stated that he understood people, that he knew people, their heroism and their cowardice. 'For twenty-five years I was at the bottom. I was at the bottom, I am at the bottom, I will be at the bottom.' His strength, then, comes from understanding people, in the most elementary situations, but also in the entire span of experience. This is how he sees himself: as a medium of the collective body, through which its life flows, but also as the co-author of the spirit of that collective body. Had he been only a passive medium, he would not, it seems, win the power to evoke faith in the future of society and hope for national greatness; he would not wield power over souls, which in Poland always turns out to be more important than material power.

Wałęsa protects his working-class identity. He is proud of being a worker. He does not want to be anything else, would not change his condition for anything. When returning from a trip to Japan, he was told at Warsaw airport that he had been awarded an honorary doctorate at Cambridge.* He was genuinely surprised, then asked suspiciously, sulking: 'As who? As a worker?' But soon he was able to enjoy his double status enormously. While Czesław Miłosz was visiting the Gdańsk shipyard, Wałęsa turned to the poet and professor, who had just been awarded an honorary doctorate by the Catholic University of Lublin: 'We will complete the work you have begun. I don't talk as nicely as you, perhaps, but – as a worker, a doctor too.' Both doctors (let us add also a third – Pope John Paul II) have captured the national imagination to an extent unheard of in Poland for decades.

Let us return, however, to the events of recent past. Workers were to be silent, or, if from time to time they were allowed to speak, it had to be according to a scenario imposed from above. Wałęsa appeared as the master of his own voice. Not as someone who adopts and imitates other people's way of speaking, but as one who uses his own unique tone. Before our eyes a triumph of 'human language', of original, free, private, individual speech, was accomplished. It coincided, of course, with the people's feel-

---

* In fact it was Alliance College, Cambridge Springs, Pa.

ings, needs, longings. And all at once tongues were loosened, all began to speak – the nation was making a great public statement.

This phenomenon often meets with reproaches: Poles are talking again! We are good only for idle talk! These endless debates will be the death of us! Those who make such charges do not understand that the essence of the shipyard workers' revolution is that they have opened their lips and regained speech. Of course, remnants of the official jargon can still be found in it. But they have tried to make full use of the 'private ownership of their throats', to use Alain Besançon's apt expression. Nothing now will be able to stifle that democratic voice! After all, democracy also means the freedom of personal expression.

Thus we have arrived at the difference between a 'worker' and a 'representative of the working class'. The first is a man who expresses himself and his brothers; the other is a gramophone record playing a recorded text.

One of the earliest written manifestations of August 1980 was a piece of paper placed on the first, temporary cross raised in front of the shipyard, marking the spot where the first dead had fallen in December 1970. On the sheet of paper, decorated with a white-and-red ribbon and a small picture of the Madonna, were the words:

> Battle for freedom
> Once begun,
> Bequeathed by father
> Passes to the Son.
> A hundred times crushed
> By the foe's might
> Still it will be won ...

It is easy to recognize here lines, well-known particularly in the romantic period but also later, from Byron's *Giaour* in Adam Mickiewicz's translation. It used to be said about Byron – in Poland – that he was the greatest British poet, so admired was he here as a bard of freedom who followed its cause to the grave, though he was much less appreciated in his own country. But these lines were written down at the shipyard somewhat differently and altered. In the original, which Mickiewicz's translation closely follows, they are:

> For Freedom's battle once begun,
> Bequeathed by bleeding sire to son,
> Though baffled oft is ever won.

At this spot, where ten years earlier blood had been shed – bloodshed which nobody remembered better than the men who had barricaded themselves into this shipyard fortress – all reference to this substance, which has always been treated as sacred in Poland, had been dropped. How is this omission to be explained? Was it a mistake, a simple oversight, or conscious intention? Was it because this revolution was already aware that it was 'self-limiting', as speakers and writers later described it? Was it because they did not want to recall then and there the blood shed in December 1970 in order not to invite revenge?

Revenge hung in the air, because the humiliation and wrong done to the people, to the entire nation, had reached their climax. I recall Mickiewicz's *Forefathers' Eve*,* performed from November 1979 at the Wybrzeże Theatre in Gdańsk, directed by Maciej Prus. Prus was a contemporary of the workers' leaders who in August 1980 were to organize the shipyard sit-in. In his production all the scenes of *Forefathers' Eve* – so different from one another – take place in a single setting: peasants taking part in an atavistic ritual are seen together with the imprisoned philomats in some deserted chapel on their way to Siberian exile. That place, though the production does not spell it out, is actually a bastion manned by a group of patriots. The people are feverish, tormented by nightmares and horrible delusions. The most oppressing is the phantasm of revenge. In *Forefathers' Eve*, as directed by Prus, the entire philomat–peasant group, in a convulsive frenzy, shouts the refrain of Conrad's 'pagan song':

> Yes! Revenge, revenge, revenge on the enemy
> With God, and even despite God! ...

The whole group, too, in the finale of the Great Improvisation, utters the unfinished phrase calling God the tsar, completing Satan's accusation that God had done wrong by allowing the crime of partitions of Poland.

---

* Forefathers' Eve (written 1823–32) by Adam Mickiewicz (1798–1855), a poetic drama whose hero is transformed from a romantic sufferer, Gustaw, into a freedom fighter, Konrad, imprisoned by the Russians with fellow 'philomats' – members of a clandestine patriotic student association at Wilno University, 1820–23.

But the lust for revenge contradicts the Christian command to be charitable and forgiving. The fantasy of a relentless struggle to win back violated national and individual rights is at odds with the equally strong dream of a chivalrous fight consistent with the highest moral ideals. The vindictive impulse of the country's defenders, ready to use any available means, conflicts with the romantic-messianic idea of the Polish ethos, whose essence consists in striving for morality in politics. Such impulses and currents ran through that theatre, or rather through life at that time.

There was a sequel. At the Gdańsk shipyard, in answer to the strikers' repeated demands, 'The Confederate Song' was mass-duplicated, without giving the name of the author. It was the entire text of the famous song of the Confederates of Bar, from Juliusz Słowacki's mystic drama, *Father Mark*.* This, one of the proudest texts in Polish poetry, begins with the words:

> Never shall we make alliance with kings,
> Never shall we bow our necks to might;
> It is from Christ we take our orders,
> Each of us Mary's knight!

'We shall not kneel before the power of authority ...' repeat the new inheritors of the idea of freedom. The proud challenge thrown to all earthly powers is combined with humble submission to spiritual powers and to moral law. In the finale of 'The Confederate Song' there is a promise and an oath:

> Hunger nor misfortune shall not break us,
> Nor the world's flattery shall lead us astray:
> For we all are the recruits of Christ,
> Each of us in His pay!

Słowacki had succeeded in capturing and re-creating that tone, which dominated the nation's struggle for freedom. It was the tone of a community seized by an ideal which was both patriotic and religious. The God of the Poles was to be the God of liberty, ever supporting its cause. After various turns, doubts and hesita-

---

* Juliusz Słowacki (1809–49), next to Mickiewicz the greatest poet of Polish romanticism. His poetic drama *Father Mark* (1843) deals with the Confederacy of Bar (1768–72), a conservative, anti-Russian and anti-Royalist movement in defence of Polish sovereignty and the privileges of the gentry. Its defeat by Russian troops after four years of guerilla warfare led to the first of the three partitions of Poland (1773).

tions, this was the conclusion eventually reached, though it had often been preceded by rebellions and loss of faith, particularly at times when God appeared to be on the side of the 'stronger battalions'. The prevailing view in Poland was that the fight for freedom was a fight for dignity, most profoundly rooted in European personalist philosophy.

Many romantic poets, who wished to write rather for the entire community than for themselves or for a small group of 'kindred spirits', treated their texts as a special form of script to be read aloud to 'the generality', 'the folk'. In this way poetry was to be transformed into life. So it turned out that 'The Confederate Song', after many years, received this further, unexpected, 'reading'. The community of workers on strike, full of religious exultation, wanted to bring themselves, their needs, their ideals, nearer to what embodied for them the Polish patriotic ethos. And so there were the inscriptions: 'GOD – HONOUR – FATHERLAND' (once embroidered on army banners), there were references to farewells to their sweetheart by freedom fighters who loved their country even more, there was the identification with insurrectionaries, knights, soldiers of freedom.

Chivalrous, religious patriotism rules out feelings of revenge and hate. It endeavours to extend nobility and magnanimity to the opponent. Wałęsa stresses he is not vindictive. During the preceding decade he had been arrested over a hundred times, but he does not call for retaliation. I think he flew into a vindictive kind of rage only once, after Solidarity activists had been beaten up by the police at Bydgoszcz.

Thus another similarity to 'myth' has emerged: to Pan Wołodyjowski, the Little Knight.* Impetuous, courageous, noble.

The August workers' movement and Solidarity, which grew out of it, have – in the eyes of participants and observers alike – one striking and distinguishing mark: they constitute above all a moral movement, a movement for ethical revival, demanding the restoration and observation of moral criteria in public and private life. This has its roots both in Christian and socialist ideals. For that matter, a long time before August 1980 the demand for 'life in

* A leading character in the trilogy of novels dealing with Polish seventeenth-century history, by Henryk Sienkiewicz (1846–1916).

truth' had been voiced in various circles. This was seen as a necessity to extricate oneself from the all-powerful lie and restore meaning to values felt and accepted by both individuals and the community as noble and honest. One could hardly miss the often religious expression of these aspirations, though the secular Left participated in them too. For how many years did one hear the saying: 'Justice went to heaven and pulled the ladder up after it'? One had to bring it back to earth.

Those aspirations have arranged themselves into a pattern, in which one can recognize certain characteristics of the Polish world outlook. I refer to those ambitions, whose origin is romantic-messianic, to bring morality into politics. One can, of course, call them naïve, or even harmful, and they have been often so called. For instance, Roman Dmowski,* to this day regarded in many quarters as a great political authority, in his book *Germany, Russia and the Polish Question*, published in 1908, declared that politics should be scrupulously separated from ethics. He stressed that 'in relations between nations there is no right and wrong, there is only strength and weakness'. He rejected very decisively the heritage of political romanticism, which had a tendency to define 'objective facts' of history in categories of 'crimes' and 'wrongs', and was convinced of the inevitable ultimate victory of 'the right cause', the sacred cause of liberty.

It is, indeed, easy to ridicule the stereotypes of romantic historical and political thinking, and point out that messianism was born, and persists, as an ideology of the weak and humiliated. Romanticism is said to compromise and destroy itself with its lack of realism, with its noble sublimity, totally cut off from life; a sublimity which must suffer one defeat after another in contact with reality. From this point of view the effort to apply moral criteria in politics, to value political actions from ethical standpoints, can be seen as the fantasies of maniacs and cranks, who have never succeeded in anything and who want to make a virtue out of their failures and disasters.

But one can look also at this phenomenon in quite a different way and see in it a shrewd intuition about the real sources of the Polish people's longings. They had been forced to become the prey

---

*Roman Dmowski (1864–1939), Polish politician and political writer, ideologist and leader of the right-wing National Democratic Party.

of aggressive forms of nationalism, founded on the separation of politics from ethics. If the Polish people did not want to answer nationalism with nationalism, they had to find another solution, to attempt to introduce moral principles as the regulators of politics. Such is the deepest sense of Polish romantic messianism, and the ideas of its founders, in different guises, appear even now, particularly in Christian circles. Recently Pope John Paul II, brought up on them, has again reminded Europe and the world of them.

In the issue of *Sztandar Młodych* for 1–3 May 1981, an interview with Wałęsa was published under the significant title 'We Can Indeed Win a Great Poland'. The dates, too, had a special significance. What did Wałęsa want to say on the workers' May Day and the national holiday of the Constitution.* First of all, he said, 'we must build on honesty'. When journalists expressed doubts, saying that 'in the long run honesty is not too strong a card in politics', Wałęsa replied with conviction: 'August has proved that it is not only a strong card, but also a real chance of salvation to reiterate that conviction. The journalists agreed that Wałęsa had 'the greatest moral right' to erect a signpost for Solidarity and asked what he would put on it. They received a laconic reply: 'Heart. Heart, truth and justice.' It is, of course, the romantic heart in which the Poles have always looked for hope.

Movements of moral restoration in politics create a danger: of seeing the world in black-and-white categories, of being unable to compromise. But this disadvantage has its advantages too – on occasions when it is necessary radically to put an end to wrongs, to divide clearly 'good' from 'evil', to restore elementary meanings to distorted and counterfeit notions.

Let us go back to the title of the *Sztandar Młodych* interview. The greatness of Poland that Wałęsa has in mind and talks about is not understood in a nationalist way, it does not proceed from the doctrine of national egoism. On the contrary, that greatness is closely connected with what Wałęsa simply calls 'honesty', 'truth', 'justice'. Polishness becomes in this way a universal idea, and

---

* 3 May is the anniversary of the reformist Constitution of 1791, commemorated as a national holiday, though not in communist Poland. It was, however, spontaneously celebrated in 1981.

Poland – a moral law. Just as in the lines of Krasiński's *Dawn*,* addressed to the ideal Poland:

> For me you are no more a land,
> A place – a home – a helping hand,
> A state that died, in ghostly awe:
> But you are Faith, but you are Law!

Having completed the editing of his film *Man of Iron*, Andrzej Wajdą admitted that August 1980 still means words more than images, signs or symbols. 'Hence the unusual success of the *Workers 80* documentary, because in it we hear what we want to hear from the screen. Now we can speak out directly, and so a film that wants to transmit the truth must use words.' And the director feels he has temporarily abandoned his original visual style.

It may be true what he says about words. But at the same time I feel that those words are not alone, isolated, empty; I feel that they are full and mature, because behind them there is a long row of symbols, just as there is behind the heart that Wałęsa was talking about. I have frequently met the view, going back to positivist ideas, that popular culture is a derivative compilation of borrowed elements. This is supposedly true of its August and post-August expressions: a rubbish dump of so-called high culture, some deformed fragments, relics, remnants. But it is not so. In fact, there emerges in front of our eyes an entity combining both working-class and national culture.

I shall recall just one phenomenon, a verbal one but also connected with an emblem. I am thinking of 'Poland Has Not Perished Yet',† sung by the shipyard workers and intoned by Lech Wałęsa. This singing became a regular practice, particularly in dangerous situations and at difficult moments. The National Anthem was transformed into a workers' song. In the striking shipyard, 'Poland Has Not Perished Yet' was sung not only to muster courage but to confirm the purpose of action and find out what to do next.

---

* Zygmunt Krasiński (1812–59), Polish romantic poet. His poem *The Dawn* was written in the years 1841–3.

† Poland's National Anthem. Composed by Jósef Wybicki in 1797, two years after the extinction of Polish independence, it became the song of the Polish legionaries who gathered in Italy under Napoleon's sponsorship in order to liberate their country.

The words 'Poland has not yet perished, while we are alive' contain a special and perpetual truth. Every generation that was, is and will be can sing 'while we are alive', and every generation is right. Always. For as long as we have had the fatherland in our hearts, Poland has not perished. In his lectures at the Collège de France, in 1842, Adam Mickiewicz said that the words of this song had inaugurated the modern history of Poland. They mean, he explained, that 'people who preserve in themselves what constitutes the essence of Polish nationality are able to prolong the existence of their fatherland independently of any political conditions, and can strive for its restoration'. He went on to say that 'no matter where a man may find himself, by the same token that he thinks, feels, and acts, he can be sure that at the very same moment thousands of his fellow-countrymen are thinking, feeling and acting like him. That invisible bond unites nationalities.'

Our modern history begins after the loss of independence not with despair, but with hope; not with a feeling of an end and downfall, but with a call for courage and victory. The life of the fatherland simply means the lives of people devoted to it. The shipyard workers made themselves, and others, aware of precisely this, in this way establishing a great symbolic continuity. For we must remember that all this happened shortly after the Sejm had 'institutionalized' the National Anthem and the national colours, allowing their use only in strictly defined circumstances and treating all other uses as a crime. To the bureaucratization of the idea of Poland the workers opposed a great, spontaneous patriotic outburst: they hung out, as a poem put it, the national flags 'without an order', and gave the powers that be to understand that they would use the National Anthem and the national emblem and the national colours when it was absolutely necessary for them – to live.

In this way we are entering the domain of symbolism, of the Royal Eagle and its soaring flight, and the white-and-red national colours. 'And you will never be white, And you will never be red, You will remain white-and-red,' wrote Gałczynski,* a poet who knew how to find words to express the most general feelings. Here he put in a nutshell the symbolic Polish duality and the unity in that duality. The combination of these two colours is inevitably

---

* Konstanty Ildefons Gałczynski (1905–53), Polish poet.

associated with the cult of freedom. When the actors of the Wybrzeże Theatre were reading Mickiewicz's *Books of the Polish Nation and the Polish Pilgrimage* to the shipyard workers on strike, their words appealed with uncanny force to the listeners, who were almost convinced that they had been written for them today. Poland speaks here in Mickiewicz's words: 'Whoever comes to me will be free and equal, because I am FREEDOM.'

This Polish gospel also praises the wisdom of 'those, who have told you the word of Freedom, and have suffered prisons and beatings; those who have suffered most are honoured; and those who seal their teaching with their death shall be saints'. These lines from Mickiewicz were recited on 26 June 1981 at the Poznań celebration to commemorate those who died in 1956, calling for 'bread and freedom'.

The cry of the workers was bloodily suppressed. It was not even allowed to be mentioned in the official annals of the history of the Polish People's Republic. The 'representatives of the working class' were called to a 'life' confined to newspaper reports in order to erase the others – the real workers – from memory and obliterate their existence. But the continuity of authentic working-class existence was not broken. The direct successors of the Poznań workers, and those of December 1970, wrote on the shipyard wall in Gdańsk, in August 1980: 'Man is born and lives free!' Again, the well-known slogan of the French revolutionary Declaration of Rights of Man and Citizen – 'Man is born and dies free' – underwent a significant and optimistic correction. In this new version it could become the knightly motto of Lech Wałęsa.

Chapter 6

On Mass Movements and Their Leaders

Roman Wapiński

The events of last year, the powerful strike movement and the foundation and development of a mass social–political movement known as 'Solidarity', make one think again about many aspects of Poland's most recent, and contemporary, history, particularly about the place occupied in that history by mass social movements. Though this is accompanied by the fear that the observations one makes may be burdened by deficiency of knowledge, superficial evaluations and excessive numbers of truisms, the importance of events tempts one and prompts reflection. It happens very rarely that a historian has the chance to observe directly crucial phenomena of such scale and social scope. Usually, when working on phenomena of this kind, he has to rely on sources recorded in the past. The temptation to express one's views is increased by additional facts. The first is connected with subjective experiences, resulting from some participation in political life. It was this particular fact that had determined my writing, early in 1971, an article published in the Gdańsk periodical *Litery*, where I tried to analyse some causes of the events of December 1970. Among other things I wrote there: 'It seems that the seventies are opening a new period in Poland's social history, a period marked not only by changes in social structure, but also in the sphere of social awareness. I am thinking here above all of the growth of awareness of the new working class, recruited mainly from the countryside. Such assessment can be supported, among others, by the fact that the point of reference in defining their place in society was no more the backward and poor village environment, but the cultural values of the urban environment. The range of their needs was not defined any more by the old social questions which had arisen in conditions of mass unemployment and backwardness. Its place began to be taken more and more clearly by a question of quite a different kind, finding its expression in attempts at improving working conditions, lessening the still visible differences in material standards between different social groups and strata. People's awareness of the social and political position they occupied had grown also. One can venture to assume that a considerable proportion of those in authority did not realize the changes that had occurred in the degree of awareness of the working class. This has been borne out by two facts. Firstly, some of them were still assessing social progress by criteria no longer valid, and displayed incompetence in managing the economic development of an already industrialized country. Secondly, they failed to take note of the increased awareness of the working class, and applied to it the same methods as those that had been used in the period when the process of industrialization had not yet been completed and most workers who had now reached a mature age had only been emerging from the countryside. In both cases, conformity to patterns established in the past had a negative effect, and caused a growing conflict between those in authority and society, mainly the working class.'

Those were neither very original nor comprehensive observations. They failed to take into account the failings of the system, but even so they seem to me worth quoting, because they signify a view of the crisis that had occurred in December 1970, an event whose importance should not be missed. In my opinion, the events which took place then on the Polish coast, from Gdańsk to Szczecin, were at the root of those collective and individual experiences which resulted in the strikes of August 1980, and in Solidarity.

The second fact which makes me voice my views is closely connected with my profession as historian. I am thinking here both of the problem of what place mass movements occupy in everyday social awareness, and the question of leaders, their role in the development of this kind of movement. The latter problem particularly is open to discussion: it is sometimes approached with a tendency to extremes, which results either in overrating the role of individuals or in negating it. Without undertaking to characterize the whole complexity of these problems, which would require a long dissertation, I will limit myself to sketching out my own attitude to them. In my view, an analysis of the past enables one to assert that there is no contradiction between appreciating the role played by individuals and seeing in mass movements a fundamental motive power of history. On the contrary, between the actions of an outstanding individual – for only such can be taken into account – and mass social phenomena there is a close interdependence. I know of no significant mass movement which would not produce a more or less outstanding leader. Nor do I know of cases where an outstanding individual would emerge without direct or indirect support in the strivings of a significant social group. I have deliberately used the term 'indirect support', because it pinpoints phenomena still partly hidden, strivings not yet quite articulate. To avoid misunderstanding it is worth adding that between the actions of individuals (leaders) and the strivings of masses there does not have to be, and on the whole is not, an ideal identity of purpose. There exists only a certain common platform, sometimes based on common interests, sometimes simply on trust, which makes it possible to assume leadership, though every historian can no doubt point to individuals who had great capabilities but owing to lack of wider social response did not play a part which enabled their potential to be revealed. Most characteristic in this respect is the fate of great inventors who were either ahead of their time and could not expect their ideas to be put into practice and general use or lived in a system unfavourable to innovations.

These remarks are in no way meant to lessen the importance of the problem, which, in gross simplification, can be reduced to the relation of a leader (or leaders) and the masses. This problem is encountered by a historian writing the biography of an outstanding individual, or by an analyst of mass social phenomena. It is enough to refer to the history of the Polish workers' movement, and the political peasant movement, and recall such names as, for example, Ignacy Daszyński, Jan Stapiński or Wincenty Witos.* Is

---

* Ignacy Daszyński (1866–1936), a co-founder and leader of the Polish Socialist Party; Jan Stapiński (1867–1946), a co-founder and one of the leaders of the Polish Peasant Party; Wincenty Witos (1874–1945), a leader of the Polish Peasant Party, three times Prime Minister in the 1920s.

it possible to imagine a book devoted to the history of the two political movements I have mentioned in which these names did not occur? One can quote many more analogous examples for the first few decades of the twentieth century, and in every case, at least with regard to the more outstanding leaders, one can discern the process of their growth in social prestige. This was helped by the fact that Poland had regained its independence and based its political system on parliamentary principles. From members of party or regional elites they became, in a natural way, thanks to authority acquired earlier, members of a national leaders' elite. I limit myself to three examples of this type of career: the already mentioned Witos, Józef Piłsudski* and Władysław Grabski.†️ Witos, one of the main peasant leaders even before the restoration of Poland's independence, became, particularly on taking the post of Prime Minister in July 1920, one of the leading political figures of the Second Republic. Piłsudski, who began his political career with activity in the illegal socialist movement, became the main founder of the Polish Legions and commander of their First Brigade; after November 1918, as Head of State and Commander-in-Chief, he became the leading politician of independent Poland and, in some measure, a symbol of its restoration. Whether or not it is right to see such a symbol in Piłsudski is something that historians might ponder over, but the question will not influence general feelings. His popularity had been built up both by white (positive) and black (negative) propagandists. Those who before the First World War had been inclined to see in him a 'bandit' engaged in guerilla actions, in the late twenties recognized him as the country's ruler. The third of the politicians I have mentioned, Władysław Grabski, is generally remembered only as the author of the monetary reform of 1924, which substituted the totally devalued Polish mark by złoty, but he too had gained his authority by his earlier participation in social and political life.

To sum up, one can, I think, see that the leading elites, which played a decisive role in the struggle for the independence and shaping of the restored Polish state, had developed in a natural way. The spontaneous formation of the leading elites was not

* See note on p. 17.
† Władysław Grabski (1873–1938), politician and economist, was a member of the National Democratic Party and Prime Minister, 1923–5.

stopped in the thirties either, though the strengthening of an authoritarian system of government played a negative role in this respect. The negative results of this system of government were felt most by the ruling circles themselves, where institutionalized, in fact bureaucratic, careers came to play a much more important role than natural careers supported by talent and social prestige. The opposition was in a better situation, but it too felt the negative results of departure from principles of parliamentary democracy. The years of the Second World War, though the political life of the country was forced to move underground, did not stop the process of forming spontaneous leading elites. Its manifestations could be seen also in the first years after liberation from the German occupation. This was favoured by the need for reconstruction, for action to establish an administration in the Regained Territories, and also, at least in the years 1945–6, by a certain plurality in political life.*

The situation changed radically in the late forties, when the effect of the minority wielding power became more marked than hitherto. Without going into the history of the Polish People's Republic, as this would require a separate study, I will limit myself to preliminary observations touching on some aspects of that history. One of them is the institutionalization of social and political life which gives preference to a bureaucratic type of career. This can be discerned not only in careers proffered by political organizations. The same situation can be seen in the sphere of economics, science, etc. Generally speaking, even when one notices some positive exceptions, one can assert that inclusion in any institutionalized leading group has been a result of nomination, promotion, decided by the approval of superiors. An additional factor which made it difficult for leaders enjoying a genuine social authority to emerge was the departure of successive groups of leaders in crisis situations. Almost invariably the removed body of leaders was charged with responsibility for economic and other failures. This

---

*The Regained Territories (or Western Territories) are the regions of the German Reich east of the Oder and Neisse rivers acquired and re-settled by Poland after the Second World War. The German population mostly fled or was expelled. 'Regained' refers to Poland's historical claim to these regions, although many of them had been overwhelmingly German in population for several centuries.

was followed by a few years at least when one tried to forget about those who were part of the removed leadership.

Those weaknesses inherent in the system were at odds with the professional and cultural advancement of the masses, and the democratization of social relations. On the one hand, in the process of institutionalized advancement, almost exaggerated attention was paid to the working-class or peasant origin of a given person; on the other, there were no conditions for natural careers. In the seventies this situation was augmented by the general trend on the part of some institutionalized leading groups to enrich themselves, to gain personal material advantages. If we add to this the consequence of generation changes, we shall fully realize why there grew in society a longing for authentic authority, morally pure and unburdened with participation in institutionalized leading groups. This longing had manifested itself many months, even years, before August 1980. It is enough to mention a considerable increase of the Church's authority, or, in another sphere, the popularity of biographies, where, in my opinion, readers looked less for models than for ideals, which would create at least an authority substitute for the present day. The lonely man in a crowd felt even more lonely because of the prevailing conditions. That too was one of the fundamental reasons why the people who had arisen as leaders of the strike movement in the summer of 1980 were accepted as authorities. They were part of that anonymous crowd, and people felt they could identify themselves with them.

The relation of society to the state is only in part a separate problem. Rule by minority; the manipulation of society, or at least endeavours in that direction; the representation of the state as something abstract, something that only the institutionalized leading groups care for; these and other factors contributed to create a state of affairs which can hardly be considered normal. The movement of working people in industry and in the countryside which grew in 1980 has been defined as the rebellion of producers. One of its fundamental causes is said to be the desire to get rid of waste. There is no doubt that, since the summer of 1980, we have been witnessing an open criticism of the many deteriorations and failings of the political and economic system; or that almost the entire active part of society has put their veto on being governed without its participation. Those are positive factors whose importance cannot be overstressed. But notwithstanding all this, the question arises whether all the basic aspects of the system have been fully discovered and assessed. I am not surprised that the package of demands put forward in August 1980 was very big, although it exceeded the capacity of our economy, and not only in that crisis year. I see it as a result of the failure of the institutionalized leading groups to fulfil the promises made earlier. Nor is the continued pressure of demand surprising, because almost all concessions by the authorities have been forced on them. At the same time, however, two weaknesses have been revealed, which to my mind are marked not only in our economy today. I stress that these weaknesses have not emerged, but been more fully revealed; their signs were evident much earlier. One of them can be seen with the naked eye: it is enough to look at the empty shops. The other, however, remains hidden, even more deeply now, perhaps, than some years ago. I see it in social egalitarianism, which we consider to be an unquestioned political achievement. Its importance has increased now, that much is certain. I do not intend to question the principle of social egalitarianism either, but as a historian I must observe that by the nature of things those principles clash with dreams of a fast, or at any rate more tangible, growth in the country's economic potential. Unfortunately, the history of economics and technology have produced evidence which does not allow for a bright outlook for the economic development of a country based on egalitarian principles.

I am a specialist not in social politics but in history, and I cannot tell which is better: the maintenance and development of the principles of social egalitarianism, or what we call material progress. I am convinced, though, that one must be aware of contradictions existing in this respect. Otherwise the hopes which society sees in the present changes may be thwarted. That would be catastrophic not only for Solidarity but also for the nation as a whole. The danger is increased by the faith of those forces in both Solidarity and the Polish United Workers Party which play the main part in the work of reconstruction rather than renewal (only what was once perfect is worth renewing). These forces represent on the whole the young generation of Poles, those least affected by the negative experiences which had been the lot of previous generations. This generation, which grew up largely after December 1970, has the courage to act and faith in its own strength, and could be the salvation of the whole country.

There remains the last question worthy of consideration. I am thinking of the experience gained through the events of December 1970. They have played a varied and very important part. I will limit myself to just three aspects. The first has been reflected in the leading part played in August 1980 by the shipyard workers. The second, in the adopted method of the struggle: in using the sit-in strike as a weapon. The third aspect may be seen through the prism of experiences of the August leaders. At least some of them had gained their first experiences in December 1970, and after ten years, a few, like Lech Wałęsa, assumed the leadership.

Chapter 7

'He Is Most Certainly a Tribune of the People'

Jerzy Kołodziejski

My first meeting with Lech Wałęsa took place at the time of the now historic event, the August strike at Gdańsk shipyard. Or more precisely on the day I went to the shipyard on behalf of the government side to define the conditions for negotiations. Earlier, news of Wałęsa had reached me in a fragmentary way.

I remember that first meeting very well. The drama of the occasion made me record numerous details in my memory. I entered the shipyard with apprehension and somewhat abashed. The thousands of people in front of the gate, the difficulty of making one's way through, the varied reception – from applause to quite violent shouting – all this was natural, but it caused great psychological tension. And it was then that our first meeting took place. Frankly, I had imagined a different man: big, hard, with a strong, determined voice and a way of behaviour signifying that he did not brook any opposition. Whereas I met a man of medium height, with an amicable smile, welcoming in a friendly manner not only the tributes of the strikers but also the representative of the authorities, myself. That friendliness, expressed in gestures, words, way of behaviour, touched me greatly at the time and evoked in me a positive response towards him. While we were walking from the shipyard gate to the place where we were to negotiate, a friendly conversation ensued, in the course of which Mr Wałęsa expressed the hope that we had to, and would, come to an agreement.

That certainty, and his attitude to me, a representative of the authorities, was very important just then. It influenced the way in which I conducted our talk and my later report to my superiors.

I went to the shipyard, among other things, to test the atmosphere, to find out who the people were with whom we would conduct the negotiations and whether there was a chance of coming to an agreement. Wałęsa was very busy just then – everyone wanted something from him. He took part in those preliminary talks only sporadically. If he butted in, it was mainly in order to stimulate confidence in the possibility, necessity, of taking up negotiations with the government commission. Thanks to him the attitude of other strike leaders was positive too. From the outset he created a favourable atmosphere for getting negotiations going.

Later there were many meetings. During the negotiations, which ended with the signing of the agreement, I observed his way of behaving and acting. Also, after the strike had ended, our meetings were frequent. They involved the settling of all conflicting matters, concerning not only Gdańsk region but also basic disputes in the country as a whole in the post-August period. In view of the physical proximity between myself, the regional party's first secretary, Tadeusz Fiszbach, and Wałęsa, we were very often approached with requests to conduct preliminary talks, establish contacts, sound views. Hence I know Wałęsa from many meetings, and I know his attitude to everything that happens in Poland.

What can I say about him, to give, as it were, a synthesis of all those meetings? He is most certainly a kind of tribune of the people, born from a genuine revolutionary movement. The movement, which later called itself 'Solidarity', was a mass movement of the working class and of society. It acted according to laws characteristic of such movements. Wałęsa was a true child of that movement, able to identify himself fully with everything it was doing, impatient, wanting to settle problems as soon as possible, at once, now, disregarding all conventions accepted by the legal or state system. Many a time I have heard him ask the questions: 'Why can't we do it? What regulations, what laws? Is it necessary? It is. Then let's do it!' Besides, he had a great capacity to adjust to the dynamics of the movement, the dynamics of events. For instance, he was not accustomed, and is not accustomed to this day, to act in an orderly and well-arranged manner. He never writes notes for himself so that he can take the floor prepared, as is done in the traditional state apparatus. I have noticed that in what he is saying one can trace some of his advisers' rationalized views, but that influence does not take roots. He utters these views, but after a time he departs from them, going back to the voice of the masses. He senses what people think. This is why I think he is a kind of people's tribune. Some say contemptuously that he is a soap-box speaker who can jump on to a platform and speak off the cuff, in a way that convinces those assembled and wins him applause. There is something in this, though I disagree with the negative attitude to this sort of action common in my circles, who are used to a more ordered type of behaviour. His actions are not like that, they are spontaneous, unconventional.

What other characteristics, arising out of his main role as tribune of the people, does Wałęsa have? First of all, he is a realist. His realism is like that of a large community. In fact, people have average needs, they know what can be afforded, and they do not ask for too much. Wałęsa is not an extremist, and even if he uses extremist slogans, in all negotiations he takes a realistic standpoint, sensing not only the needs but also the possibilities of the other side. His realism is masked by cunning. He is cunning. At the start of negotiations he takes a stance, usually a maximalist one, but he regards it only as a point of departure. He does not insist that what he proposes, and only that, must be accepted. In this he differs from many of his collaborators who, from beginning to end, without regard to circumstances, possibilities or changes in the situation, stick to their original view, unaltered. His is certainly the realism of the class he comes from, and with which he feels himself bound up. He is – very important, this – open to the views of others. That open attitude allows him to change his view under the influence of arguments. I have noticed that some views which he at first rejects can on consideration be built into his own stand.

That open attitude leads to his continuous development and improvement, which is very important for a politician. If one compares the Wałęsa of August 1980 to the Wałęsa of August 1981, one sees that they are two different people. Through his open attitude and his realism, he has changed, has matured politically; he has become a politician who not only discerns the needs of the current situation but looks forward. He is helped in this by his natural capacity to sense things; he has a political 'nose', a political instinct. All this shapes in him something which counts a great deal in politics: imagination. In this respect, too, he has gained a lot since August

1980. He does not think only in present-day terms any more, but he can get ahead of reality and gear his current behaviour to future events. I could give numerous examples of this, but I would not wish to expose him. In his political calculations these may be matters of some importance. I think they are.

When I say that Wałęsa develops as a politician, he is no doubt helped in this by his diligence. He is an unusually hard-working man. It can easily be seen that he has been the most widely travelled of all politicians in the post-August period. Has anyone been to so many parts of Poland in such a short time as Wałęsa, all in the course of his ceaseless political activity? In social conflicts, he has acted, as he himself says, in the capacity of a fireman, constantly on the move. In maintaining contacts with people he is helped by his great friendliness. He is friendly. And people sense both his friendliness and his opposition to all that is wrong. At the same time, he generates optimism. I have observed him at the shipyard and in many tense situations: his optimism has never left him. Sometimes his optimism is the result of too superficial an analysis of events and their causes. On the other hand, when I think of people like myself, I come to the conclusion that we approach in too rationalistic a way phenomena that are irrational in themselves. And this is the reason for Wałęsa's superiority over us. He grew up with this movement and knows its laws. And he knows very well that intuition and feeling are more important than cool analysis, which reduces everything to the smallest elements and then aims at synthesis, often too late. And it turns out that it is people like Wałęsa who are right, not we. They assess the situation better.

I remember a telephone conversation with him in March 1981. He was on his way to Bydgoszcz, where the situation looked tragic.* He was full of optimism. 'I will deal with it,' he said. I was convinced he would not succeed. On the basis of available facts I thought that the situation had been so inflamed, the conflict had grown so acute, that there was no possibility of de-fusing it. But it turned out he had not been boasting. By means known only to himself he was able to smooth things out.

Some people think he lacks consistency, that he is changeable

---

* Relations between Solidarity and the authorities reached a point of crisis on 19 March 1981, when police forcibly evicted Solidarity strikers from the prefecture at Bydgoszcz and beat several of them up.

in his views, even perfidious. That he does not abide in one place by what he has decided in another. One can discern something like that, though to my mind this is not caused by a trait in his character, but is only a result of the instability of political ideas in the movement he leads. For that matter, it is very difficult to have any stability in such dynamic times. The charge of perfidiousness, made by some people, is caused by an inability to understand the fact that Wałęsa, while sensing a mood exactly, in order to retain credibility in his own environment cannot speak a different language from those whom he represents. I have often heard reproaches: You talk to him, come to an understanding, and then he mounts the platform and says something different. When I hear this, I reply: But does he achieve his aim? Yes, they could retort, but because of all kinds of outside factors. I do not agree with this. He has the capacity of flexible action, using different ways of behaviour depending on the situation, without, however, losing sight of the aim he wants to reach. And if we take the whole post-August period into account, the balance is to Lech Wałęsa's advantage. He is really representative of a moderate, middle-of-the-road line, avoiding extremes. This demands constant balancing acts from him. On the one hand, he has within Solidarity a very radical group supported by and appealing to public opinion. On the other hand, he has some obscure people whose views he cannot take into account either if he wants to be representative of a social movement. He knows how to keep the golden mean and in this sense is in accord with the line supported by our current political doctrine – the line of social agreement.

I have concentrated on Wałęsa's positive qualities, and have not mentioned any negative ones. I wonder if he has any? Certainly, if, having all the attributes of a people's tribune, he had a deeper intellectual base – education – he would be an even better politician. He says himself that he is hampered by his lack of education. It hampers him in the deeper understanding of social and political phenomena. But this is also a weakness of the movement he leads. That movement as a whole is not prepared to carry the burden it has taken on itself, either organization- or education-wise. The fact is, however, that Wałęsa can turn even a failing to his advantage. Oriana Fallaci asked him in an interview what books he had read in his life. He replied nonchalantly that he had not read any book from beginning to end. He could afford such an answer, knowing it would not harm him. There was also in this reply a certain cunning which – it seems to me – Fallaci did not grasp. People are a bit fed up with all those professors, clever men who take the country from one crisis to another. There is something like that in the social psyche and mood, and he senses it. The devil take all those intellectuals, let us take care of our problems, in our simple peasant way; no big brains are needed here. How has this attitude appeared? It comes from the fact that distortions and deformations have happened on such a wide scale that even the simplest things are not functioning. And so people say that it is not intellect that is needed but common sense. Wałęsa senses this. He says sometimes: Most of all I do not like talking to professors, for once they begin to advise and complicate things, I get lost in it all, and nothing comes of it. But I remember Wałęsa's attitude and words which prove that the common-sense trend in him is superficial, and that deep down he favours a rational way of thinking.

In August 1980 there were arguments whether expert advisers should take part in the talks. And it was Wałęsa who at that time was firmly for their inclusion. He said: We must rely on people who have knowledge, we cannot cope alone, we are only simple workers. He puts forward this thesis often: 'I'm a worker and don't have to know all the complexities; I must know what the workers want; but how to settle their demands, this is a problem for those who know these things'. It must also be said that in August Wałęsa did take into account the formulas prepared by these advisers. In the conditions then prevailing at the shipyard few people thought it necessary. This applied particularly to the package of demands which amounted to a political declaration being included in the agreement. The strikers were not concerned about a distant future and how the agreement would function in the normal social–political life of the country.

During the later, very difficult talks, particularly those with Prime Minister Pińkowski, I noticed that Wałęsa was relying on advisers, while trying to maintain both caution and independence with regard to them. And here I return to the tribune of the people, for whom the most important thing will always be what people say and expect. A feedback occurs here. Wałęsa knows he is a somebody thanks to the support given him by the masses. For this reason it is the contact with the masses that is the most important for him, a contact he cannot maintain through intermediaries or representatives. Hence his meetings at sports stadiums and in big halls. He told me once that he feels the crowd. He alters his speeches while looking people in the eyes. We know, if only from diaries of leaders, that in other revolutionary movements, the Russian revolution, for example, it was very important to sense the mood of the assembly, the atmosphere of the crowd. Wałęsa is so attached to this style of action that no promoters are able to deflect him from his main line of behaviour. It is interesting to note that after periods of intimate staff meetings, as it were, when one does not hear much about Wałęsa, he feels the need to refresh himself through contact with people.

Is there something he does not appreciate enough? Well, the need to strengthen the organizational structure of Solidarity. An organization of ten million people cannot function only as a social movement, in a spontaneous kind of way. Wałęsa, it seems to me, is afraid of institutionalization, of bureaucracy. He fears that such a bureaucratic system would separate him from the people. On the other hand, he will not master such a powerful movement by the method of direct contact, direct meetings and assemblies. There must exist an efficient organizational structure. People cannot be bound together only through the building-up of drastic situations. Until now this has been tactics, a formula. But to keep Solidarity together in the long run, one must substitute for this method an efficient organization based on rational foundations. This is the law of any revolution. As we know from history, a revolutionary mood cannot be maintained for long periods. Revolution must be accomplished. But once it has been accomplished, other methods of human activity must be sought. I think that Wałęsa, endowed with political instinct and political imagination as he is, in becoming a more mature politician will discern and appreciate that necessity in time.

Prepared from notes by Edmund Szczesiak

Chapter 8

'Be Great, Mr Wałęsa'

Grzegorz Fortuna

We have lived to see the appearance of a new and great public figure: his name is Lech Wałęsa. That is how one can best sum up, in a sentence, the gist of the letters which have been sent to the leader of Solidarity. But as one reads those letters one can't help thinking that there is more to it than that. That one is dealing here with a social myth which is beginning to grow and envelop the union's leader.

The letters usually start off fairly conventionally. The equivalent forms in English of 'Szanowny Panie Wałęsa', 'Szanowny Panic Lechu', 'Panie Wałęsa' at the top of the letters might be given as 'Dear Mr Wałęsa', or 'Dear Sir'. But a fair number begin quite differently. 'My dear son', 'To the highly esteemed Lech Wałęsa', 'My dearest Lech' or 'To the Outstanding Pole of 1980' are not at all uncommon.

The letters then go on to give opinions and impressions, assessments and requests. Lech Wałęsa is a great man. 'Mr Wałęsa, I consider you to be second only to God Himself, here on this earth, of course ... Mr Wałęsa, I look upon you as the liberator of the Polish workers and farmers, I look upon you as a Great National Hero, Mr Wałęsa' (Kielce province). 'I'd like to start my letter with the words: A man of the people will perform a miracle' (Warsaw).

He is so great that comparisons come spontaneously. 'There are very few people of your stature in Poland today and I don't know them all by name. Of those whose names I do know, I'll mention them all: Wojtyła, Wyszyński, Wałęsa. Their names all begin with the letter W'* (Zakopane). 'They presented you with the traditional Tatra Highlander's hat and *ciupaga*† like they did to Pope John Paul II when he was here eighteen months ago' (Białystok province). 'I would be very grateful if you could sign the enclosed sheet of paper so I can add it to my personal collection of autographs. I already have the autographs of Pope John Paul II, Cardinals Wyszyński, Rubin and Macharski, the composers Penderecki and Lutosławski, the actress Helena Modzelewska, the singers Kiepura Ładysz, the astronaut Hermaszewski and many others. It would be a great privilege for me to have the autograph of Mr Lech Wałęsa, too' (Prague). 'This branch of the Kashubian–Pomeranian Association in conjunction with the parish of Lębork request the pleasure of your company at a performance of our Nativity Play in which you and the Pope are the chief characters.'

Wałęsa gives life a sense of purpose. 'Maybe I was being a bit sentimental although I was certainly very sincere when I said once – this was at a meeting of our circle – that if you let us down, Mr Wałęsa, you as a human being, that is, then life wouldn't be worth living any more because you have to believe in something in this world in order to live. Since you're a fervent Catholic, a statement like that probably makes you very angry. But personally, I've got to have something over and above my faith in God: I've got to believe in people as well if I'm going to have enough strength to carry on this struggle with life' (Warsaw).

Wałęsa is deserving of all manner of distinctions, honour, respect and esteem. 'I heard that you are in the running for the Nobel Prize. I would be very well pleased if that did happen because you deserve to get all the prizes there are in the world' (Bydgoszcz province). 'I don't know what you union leaders are up to now, but I'd like to say just one thing: you must respect Mr Lech Wałęsa. The Pope himself respects him, and the whole Church and the world does, too. Pope John Paul II welcomed him in St Peter's capital and bestowed the highest honours on him that are only ever bestowed on crowned heads' (Gdańsk province). 'I sincerely hope you get that Nobel Prize. It would be the first prize ever for a worker' (Łódź province). '... without a word of exaggeration I can describe you as a Saviour' (Silesia).

---

*Like '*wielki*', the Polish word for 'great'.   † A decorated stick.

Wałęsa is the embodiment of fundamental human values. He is well-nigh omnipotent and yet, for all his extraordinary aggrandizement, he remains very close to the people. 'You, the Leader of the Independent Trade Union Solidarity as they call you now, want to create goodness and prosperity for the working man ... At the moment all I can do is let you know about my complaints because you're a man who understands about justice and I've been looking for justice for years now and I still haven't found any' (Białystok province). 'Please speak out on the television and jolt the nation's conscience; please stir their hearts and may the Lord God Almighty and the Queen of Poland, Mary, Mother of God, help you' (Katowice).

Very often, people confide in Wałęsa in their letters. All sorts of people describe their hard and sometimes tragic lot, convinced that he is the one person who can help them and set them free. This trust and belief that Wałęsa represents the ideals of a caring and, at the same time, a fulfilling compassion are of a very intimate nature. That is why I have refrained from quoting the relevant extracts.

Solidarity's leader is a man who, by his own actions, satisfies a craving for fundamental human values. 'All the things that are happening in Poland now are of great value and importance. They are unique. I am aware of the significance of the free trade unions which have been created; I am aware of the significance of the remaining twenty demands made by Gdańsk and the other towns. But to me there is something far more important even than that, something quite different. Following August 1980 the name of Lech Wałęsa, worker, has been written into the history books of Poland (and probably not just of Poland, either). If you look at it closely, the history of the sixties and the seventies has been made by our "leaders": first secretaries, prime ministers and the occasional professor or writer. And now they have been joined by a worker who could, and did, think for himself. A worker who had enough courage to give voice to his views and convictions openly. And that was enough to get the whole of Poland talking about him – to get nearly the entire world talking about him, in fact.

'You have shown us that we mustn't be frightened off by police truncheons, nor by ridicule, nor lack of understanding. The other thing that really impresses me is your profound faith. I'm a

Catholic myself and I've never concealed it. But I must admit that
I was very moved indeed when I saw a cross hanging on the wall
during the talks with the government; and you had a rosary and
a picture of Our Lady of Częstochowa on you. Even today when
I remember those photographs, or the fragments of the Holy Mass
that was celebrated in the shipyard and transmitted by Swedish
television, my spine tingles and my eyes fill with tears of emotion.
Those moments were truly unforgettable. I would like to thank
all the people who were at those Masses – may Heaven reward you'
(Kraków).

Wałęsa's religious faith prompts avowals like these: 'I am quite
sure that the man who fights under the banner of the Cross and
who approaches the Lord's Table often, that the man who carries
the picture of Our Lady of Częstochowa on his breast will triumph.
He will triumph because history has been teaching us for twenty
centuries that those who fought against the laws of God were
vanquished' (Łódź province). 'We all love you and bless you and
we pray for you. We pray for Poland and we pray for you in the
same breath. Only don't make it difficult for our prayers to be
heard. You must take a rest sometimes' (Kraków).

Occasionally questions like: 'Why, as a brother-Catholic, don't
you visit the sick in hospital?' appear in the letters. And sometimes
there are sombre warnings. 'You must believe that all true Poles
are behind you whole-heartedly. That puts a heavy responsibility
on you, and you must not let them down' (Lower Silesia). One
writer asks him to respect his family's privacy, many others advise
him to give up smoking. The Larousse encyclopedia asks him for
personal data for their next edition.

It is extremely rare for the letters to be written in the very
formal, bureaucratic language using the second person plural in
preference to the more traditional third person singular.* But even

* In Polish, it is customary to address strangers or acquaintances who are not close friends
or colleagues as 'pan' (male), or 'pani' (female). Because 'pan' has connotations with
'lord' (in addition to the neutral 'mister'), bureaucratic and particularly Party speech
after the war tended to avoid the use of 'pan/pani' and reverted to the use of the second
person plural form when dealing with strangers or in official correspondence. This form,
'wy', is an old Polish dialect form. It is also, however, standard Russian usage, and it is
that which makes it so unappealing to Poles. Only one of the letters quoted here uses this
form; all the others use the traditional form of the third person singular 'pan' when
addressing Wałęsa.

then, the sentiments are clear. 'It is hard to express just how much you are doing for Poland and for the world. You are a Sign of the Times' (Sweden). And in a letter to Mrs Wałęsa, another writer says: 'He is so important to us! I don't know if you realize just how many people love and adore him. I am a fanatical worshipper of the chairman. I would gladly tear anyone who dared to say anything bad about Mr Wałęsa into little pieces. But people like that are just simpletons or downright evil' (Łódź).

There are also some extremely antagonistic and even hate-filled letters. Their minimal quantity, however, only emphasizes the vastness of the myth which is beginning to surround the leader of the union. When I use the word 'myth' I have no intention of diminishing Wałęsa's merits, or of disparaging his significance. When he welcomed Miłosz at the Catholic university in Lublin, Father Rector Krąpiec spoke of the crystallization of symbols 'which the entire nation experiences in the shape of real-life people'. Though he was talking about Miłosz, could not his words apply equally well to Wałęsa?

In the view of the correspondent Wałęsa's greatness stems from the fundamental values which he is reckoned to conform to and represent. Courage, integrity, dignity, honesty, compassion verging on omnipotence, moral rectitude combined with profound religiousness, heroism, veracity, sincerity – the list of qualities could be extended almost indefinitely. The picture they paint is very one-sided and, in a sense, even quite sparse. But the letters do paint another picture – that of their writers, the inadvertent creators of a myth. People for whom the values mentioned above really are important and worthy of respect. They are aware that an opportunity has arisen and they believe that those values can be resurrected and accepted once more as important and immutable. Protesting against the system which has been in force, they put all their hopes into something which is diametrically opposed to it. Into something which has enabled them to express their opposition, something which has, in fact, made it possible for that opposition to come into being. The myth of Wałęsa is, therefore, a myth which springs from opposition. But it is also a by-product of the very system against which the movement he leads is directed.

The system of social corruption, progressive demoralization and omnipresent frustration was alien to those people. They tolerated it because there was a threat of repression hanging over them. But the joviality of the political and social leaders was alien to them; the self-proclaimed leadership of state and nation was alien to them, and the unilaterally pronounced moral and political unity in the country was alien.

Wałęsa, on the other hand, is one of them. His speech is rough and straightforward. He is not afraid to make natural gestures that come from the heart. He has the courage to be himself regardless of where he finds himself. He probably has an exceptional intuitive gift which means that he never hurts people's feelings by being overbearing or stand-offish. He is protected, too, by a charisma which is both astounding and manifestly simple. Its source can be found, among other qualities, in those aspects of his character which make people think of him as just 'an average man in the crowd'. Every single person can walk up to him and shake him by the hand, or they can write to him and tell him what has upset them and how they've been hard done by. Every man and woman can address him by his first name. The myth of Wałęsa is a myth of homeliness which is in sharp contrast to the alien nature of the system.

Like all myths, that of Wałęsa is created, in part, by hyperbole. Lately, various analysts have started to search for Romantic themes in the Polish upheavals. Georges Poulet, writing about the Romantics' conception of time, expressed the opinion that exaggeration was the single most important element making up the Romantic soul. And, to some extent, the Wałęsa myth is wrapped by this emotional cloak; for the protest is not just a cry in support of values, it is also a cry in support of feelings. It is inspired by a yearning not just for values and for a leader who will personify them, but also for straightforward, unequivocal feelings that haven't been subjected to unnecessarily discursive manipulations. Adoration, affection, devotion, loyalty – this list, too, could be extended almost indefinitely – all those feelings intensified extraordinarily by hyperbole, just as exaggeration occasionally intensifies some feelings of hatred.

Homeliness, then, is its material, opposition and hyperbole are the tools which bring it into being, and we ourselves are the potential co-creators of this myth.

It has stridden into the national pantheon. The yardsticks used to make evaluations continue to be of the highest order and any potential criticism is magnified into an affront.

I am not against Wałęsa. I am not against hope. But I am against escaping from thought. I don't want the unity of the nation which, until very recently, had been proclaimed from above to be replaced by a unity about Wałęsa. In the past, opposition to the system was considered to be an anti-state activity. In the near future, opposition to Wałęsa could well be regarded as an activity aimed against those values which he is deemed to personify. I do not want programmatic atheism to be replaced by patriotic and, occasionally, religious exaltation. I do not want promises to be thought of as being the same as possibilities which can come into being at any moment. I don't want one more myth to take the place of reality. And yet that is exactly what we are doing. We are determinedly creating a myth by writing letters and articles, by performing feats of amazing manipulation on values and feelings. If we are to avoid becoming like those tossing souls whom Democritus described as being neither stable nor happy, then we must restore normality and balance.

Wałęsa wants to serve. That is what he has said on more than one occasion. The myth that is being created cannot, therefore, be to his liking: a ruler might have need of it – but a servant has none.

Chapter 9

*Wałęsa's Role in August 1980
(Extracts from Memoirs)*

In the middle of November 1980 the Gdańsk section of the Polish Sociological Association asked people to record and send in their recollections of the events in August 1980. The response, in terms of the amount of material sent in and the quality of its contents, proved to be very valuable indeed. We received 277 sets of memoirs which constitute a priceless piece of sociological and historical documentation. Wałęsa is mentioned quite frequently in a large number of the memoirs submitted.

Biographical snippets

The shipyard workers in Gdańsk are led by a young worker, an electrician by trade, who had been sacked by the management after the 'bread riots' of 1970. He is thirty-six years old, the father of six children, and he's called Lech Wałęsa. When he was freed by the police on 16 August, he went straight from the station to the shipyard.

No. 81, male, aged sixty, Legnica

Another thing that surprised me was that nobody had heard of this Lech Wałęsa, the chairman of the Strike Committee, nor about his being persecuted.

No. 77, male, pensioner, aged seventy-seven, Kraków

We're being gnawed by frustration and curiosity about this man Lech Wałęsa. Is it true he's an electrician with a pile of kids?

No. 231, female, chemist, aged thirty-three, Toruń

Wałęsa Through Local Eyes

Lech Wałęsa when still relatively unknown

After director Gniech had given his brief explanations, this Leszek W. appeared again. He, too, climbed up on to the bulldozer and told us he'd got in over the fence. I'm certain it was the first time that most of the workforce standing round that bulldozer had set eyes on Leszek. After all, it had been quite a time now since he'd been dismissed from the yard. Some of the people started asking who the fellow with the moustache was. Leszek took over the leadership of the strike. He wanted a reply to our demands and he insisted that A. Walentynowicz be allowed into the shipyard.* Leszek W. reached decisions very quickly though I must say that, to begin with, he appeared to be very tense indeed – I thought so, anyway. Leszek W. announced that all the sections would choose their own representatives to serve on the strike committee. The committee would start operating forthwith and would go to the conference hall with director Gniech. The workforce was to re-assemble at a specified time to hear what the response of the management and the authorities might be. We assembled again at one in the afternoon and A. Walentynowicz was brought in. However, the explanations we were given proved unsatisfactory. Then Leszek proclaimed a sit-in strike which would last indefinitely. Only a small percentage of the workforce went home ...

I remember clearly how, on the second day of the strike, Leszek W. spoke through the microphone at No. 2 Gate and said: 'I will keep the workers of the shipyard informed of any important developments through this microphone here by No. 2 Gate. When the time comes, I will announce the end of the strike through this microphone at No. 2 Gate.'

There were no great changes or any conclusive decisions from the management during the second day. The Strike Committee started talks with the management between nine and ten o'clock. A large part of the workforce gathered outside the conference hall, reacting to the management's announcements and greeting Leszek

*The dismissal of Anna Walentynowicz had been one of the management's more un-popular decisions in the days prior to the strike.

Wałęsa with an ovation. They sang 'A Hundred Years' for Leszek*
and then they sang the National Anthem.

... On the third day of the strike ... in the afternoon, the
agreement was signed. The shipyard workers were supposed to
leave the compound by six o'clock ... I saw Leszek W. at No. 2
Gate. He was up on an electric truck and he was exhorting the
people; he was explaining that they must stay in the yard, that we
had to continue the strike as a sign of solidarity with the other
factories and plants in the Three Towns (Gdańsk, Gdynia and
Sopot). I'm sorry to have to say that when Leszek asked the workers
who were on their way out to stay in the yard, they didn't listen.
They poured out like a river. I'll never forget that sight, or the
workers' indifference. But Leszek's appeals did bring some results.
People started to stop at No. 3 Gate and, after a while, some
started to go back to their sections. But there were very few of
them ... In the evening Leszek came down to us and we all swore
that we would stay there for as long as it took ... Monday,
18 August ... Leszek came down to No. 2 Gate at six. We sang
the National Anthem and 'Boże, coś Polskę'.† And then Leszek
chatted with us for a bit. Another ordinary strike day had started ...
All the days from the 20th right to the end had exactly the same
timetable. I'd be at No. 2 Gate by six, we'd all sing the National
Anthem and 'Boże, coś Polskę' – Leszek always took part in the
singing. From time to time there'd be rumours that some section
leaders were forcing people to go back to work. Whenever that
happened Leszek would pick up a flag and climb up onto the
electric truck. Then he would lead the rest of us in a procession
round the yard, making sure that there were no blacklegs.

On 31 August, at about five in the afternoon, Leszek Wałęsa
came to No. 2 Gate. We welcomed him with smiles and cheers.
In a short speech he explained that the strike was finished. Then
the gates were thrown open as wide as they could go ...

No. 183, male, worker in the Lenin shipyard, aged fifty, Gdańsk

---

*The Polish equivalent of 'For He's a Jolly Good Fellow' wishes the subject a hundred
years of health and good fortune.

† A hymn of great emotional significance to Poland, dating from the times of the partitions. In it the Poles ask God to give them back a free country. The secular authorities
after the war considered its sentiments inappropriate and it was never aired officially until
after the happenings of August 1980.

It was at that very moment that I heard Lech Wałęsa say we'd got what we'd wanted and the strike was over ... Minutes later a new strike as an act of solidarity was announced.

No. 264, male, worker in the Lenin shipyard, aged twenty-nine,
Gdańsk

A few yards away some man was making a speech. He was of medium height, thirtyish, with a thick moustache and hair combed back ... I saw him again on Monday in the conference hall of the Health and Safety building, and it was then I found out that the man was Lech Wałęsa ... He said we should all join in and sing 'Boże, coś Polskę' and the National Anthem ... Twenty minutes later we heard Lech Wałęsa's voice come booming out over the whole yard: he sent greetings to the workers of the North Yard who had joined the strike in an act of solidarity. He said that the men from the repair yard were supposed to have come at 8.30, but they hadn't appeared yet. After that he urged us to form a strike committee and to elect one delegate from each section ... When Wałęsa appeared (in the hall of the Health and Safety building) the entire workforce rose to its feet and sang 'A Hundred Years' in his honour. Reporters started jostling each other in an effort to push their microphones towards him, and there was a continuous glare of white light coming from the flashlights. Every sentence he uttered was greeted with applause.

No. 113, male, worker in the Northern shipyard, aged
twenty-two, Kolonia village

Wałęsa said that if the government refused to send anyone to talk to us, and if we didn't get some kind of agreement, then other plants would come out on Monday, too.

'Who is this fellow Wałęsa?' 'What do you mean? Don't you know? He's the Chairman of the Strike Committee over in the Lenin yard.' 'Well how am I supposed to know that? His name wasn't on any of the leaflets ...'

No. 266, male, fireman in the Paris Commune shipyard,
aged twenty-two, Gdynia

Straight away, almost, a man came up to us and said there was an Interworks Strike Committee being formed. He said that at least two people from our yard ought to stay on if, of course, we agreed to join the MKS (Interworks Strike Committee). We didn't know what to think. We didn't know if some of our people should stay or not, we didn't even know who we were having the pleasure of talking to. It was only later that we discovered it was Lech Wałęsa ... we used a tape-recorder, and this meant that the workers could sense the atmosphere in the conference hall, where the MKS was, more accurately. Soon they began to recognize the voices of the individual members of the MKS praesidium, and especially the voice of Lech Wałęsa.

No. 187, male, Nauta repair yard in Gdynia

Episodes from the strike

It's true, there are leaflets being printed in our place, too, but they're being put out by the official Unity Front and they're being dropped all over the shipyard. Apparently Wałęsa ordered a bonfire to be made out of the official leaflets because, he said, they were making the shipyard untidy.

No. 190, male, compositor, aged forty, Gdańsk

When there was a pause in the speech I pulled his trouser-leg to attract his attention. I didn't know who it was: he was standing on the truck with a microphone in his hand. All I knew was that everyone called him Leszek. He asked me if there was anything I wanted ...

No. 193, female, storeroom worker, aged twenty-six, Sopot

When I reached Mr Lech Wałęsa I presented him with some pink carnations which had a beautiful fragrance. He took both my hands in his. Our eyes and our hearts met. Lech Wałęsa passed me the microphone. I said: 'The teachers of Gdańsk are in solidarity with the shipyard workers.'

No. 259, female, pseudonym 'Rainbow', Gdańsk

Everyone is being kept informed about what is happening in the Gdańsk shipyard through the loudspeakers. For several days now a Government Commission and the Strike Committee, led by Lech Wałęsa – a man loved by the entire nation – have been conferring together ...

No. 121, female, pensioner, aged sixty-eight, Gdynia

Suddenly, all the cameras turned to the gate where a short man had just appeared ... It was Lech Wałęsa. I had never seen him before. He greeted the crowds on both sides of the railings. He made the sign of solidarity (two tightly clenched hands).

No. 4, male, primary school teacher, aged twenty-five, Gdańsk

Suddenly, Lech Wałęsa appeared on the roof of a building in the shipyard. The crowd fell silent and his voice became quite audible. He told us about the day's talks with the Government Commission. He speaks with feeling, and his manner is decisive. He finished his account with the words: 'We will hold out' ... And so, at last, I had seen Lech Wałęsa with my own eyes. I had seen the leader of a movement which had carried with it the working masses of the country.

No. 101, male, pseudonym 'Szczepan', technician, Malbork

The strike starts to draw to a close

The MKS, under Lech Wałęsa's leadership, is doggedly loosening the links of the chain which is barring the road to justice ... On their side of the table are ordinary people, without a great deal of learning ... led by an ordinary person dressed in a modest grey suit and wearing a rosary, the symbol of victory, at his breast.

No. 92, male, fireman in the Gdynia Port Authority, aged forty-one, Gdynia

Right to the very end we were afraid that there might be some sort of provocation. After all, if they'd signed, why was there no broadcast to tell us so? Why was there no speech from Wałęsa? And how would we know if they put someone else in his place, an actor who could imitate the MKS's leader? Mind you, that would have been fairly unlikely. Wałęsa's got a very individual way of speaking ... And then, at last, we heard Wałęsa's rough, stammering voice, so different to the smooth, monotonous, woolly speeches of the people in authority. That's why, for all its ugliness, that voice sounds beautiful ... The victory that's been achieved was a victory of will-power. There's no doubt that Wałęsa's got grit in him. And, apart from his will-power, he's got the pride of a 'Romantic hero'. It may be tilting at windmills, but it will give rise to a legend, just as Piłsudski's tilting at windmills, his raid into Kielce,* gave birth to a legend, too.

No. 195, male, docker in the Gdynia Port Authority, aged
forty-three, Gdynia

Quite often a decisive, husky voice will butt in. 'That's Wałęsa,' a neighbour tells me. So that's Wałęsa ... I nod. He doesn't find words easily, but he takes pains to stick to the point under discussion ... This man Lech Wałęsa interests me enormously. After all, he's carrying an enormous weight on his shoulders. What does he look like? What does he do? His hoarse voice almost bursts the microphone. He is homely, stubborn, and he wants everything to be precise and clear ... The cameras are all aimed at this man as he reads, quite dreadfully but forcefully, fiercely and emphatically. He uses lofty words but they are unequivocal and clear words ... Now, at last, I know what Wałęsa looks like ... Wałęsa wipes the sweat from his face using the same gesture that my brother does, a gesture I've loved since I was a child. That finally wins this man to my heart.

No. 179, male, historian, aged twenty-nine, Gdańsk

Lech Wałęsa was speaking. He was terribly hoarse. I liked his straightforward, direct way of speaking. It was a bit rough to my ears, but it really was so clear. Quite right, too: why should he have to make pretty-sounding speeches? He's not a polite 'lady', he's not a diplomat. He's not reading that to flatter us or charm us. That's what people were saying. He's a worker, not a namby-pamby intellectual. He gives it to us straight from the shoulder instead of decking it out with flowery phrases ...

Wałęsa knew how to win people over. 'My dear people ... If God is with us, then who can thrive against us?' That and similar quotes from the strike speeches really got to my mother and ... she had to borrow my hanky ... 'Lech' was surrounded by lots of young boys, and they treated him like their leader. I mean, a lot of those boys were my age. Where did their enthusiasm spring from? There must be something in it ... At the gate we looked

---

* Piłsudski launched the final phase of the struggle for independence in 1914. His policy was to exploit the war which had broken out between the three empires which had partitioned Poland. On 6 August 1914, Piłsudski and a small detachment of insurrectionaries marched into the Russian-held zone of Poland and managed to occupy the town of Kielce.

for the speaker ... Leszek believes that the demands will be met. No problem. Leszek keeps a firm grip of everything. But the most important thing is that he is one of us. And he has the gift of the gab, though he's a bit too coarse-grained for some of the more delicate listeners.

... They're clapping Leszek. There's no way that people will leave yet. They are clapping and chanting: 'Leszek! Leszek!' ... The shipyard workers are shouting: 'Lech! Let's see you, Lech! The people want to see you, Lech!' He appears. He climbs up on to the gate. His mates hold his legs so he won't fall. He speaks. He's hoarse, but happy. He promised that he would be the last to leave the shipyard and he has kept his word.

No. 261, female, office-worker, aged nineteen, Gdynia

Reactions to Wałęsa outside the Three Towns

Wałęsa signs the historic agreement

It was the first time they'd seen the leader of the strike. Lech Wałęsa read a few sentences from a piece of paper – he stammered a bit. It was obvious he wasn't a professional speaker. But you could see he was a serious man even though he was still young. He was very committed to the renewal of our society ... 'We want Poland to be a powerful state, we want to manage our own national production' – that's what Wałęsa said.

No. 258, female, worker in the state administration, aged fifty-seven

I listened to Lech Wałęsa's words very carefully ... though I can't remember the exact quotation I did compare his words with those uttered a hundred years ago, during the Turkish occupation, by the Bulgarian national hero, Vassil Levski. He said: 'If I win, the whole nation will win. If I lose, I will lose only myself.' I'm not sure if that quotation is appropriate, but that is what Wałęsa's speech made me think of at the time.

No. 31, female, resident of Bulgaria

And then Wałęsa spoke. He expressed his gratitude to the Deputy Prime Minister and said that thanks to him and a small group of sensible people the agreement had been reached without resorting to force to settle the dispute (that's how the press and the television put it). Later, though, the censors crossed out the bit about 'a small group of sensible people' in the press here. It must have touched all those numerous opponents of agreements with the workers.

No. 75, male, pensioner, aged seventy-two, Kraków

Lech Wałęsa's speech was completely different from the speech made by the Deputy Prime Minister which turned out to be the speech of an experienced diplomat, which Jagielski undoubtedly is.

No. 103, male, engineer, aged fifty-one, Lisewo Malborskie, Elbląg province

The strikes are over. Lech Wałęsa has signed an agreement with the government. We watched it on the television in silence, deeply moved ... As you watched the last moments, when they were putting their signatures under the joint agreement, you just wanted to hug them as if they were your own sons whom you love overwhelmingly.

No. 167, female, nurse, aged twenty-five, Lublin

The first time I met Wałęsa was in the evening. The speeches bringing the strike in Gdańsk to an end were very moving, particularly Wałęsa when he spoke in simple, unadorned language about how 'a Pole can always talk to another Pole'.

No. 242, female, higher education teacher, aged thirty, Szczecin

... In the late afternoon, through the wide-open gate, a car, carrying Mr Lech Wałęsa and his entourage, drove out. People were giving him an ovation. Flowers were being handed to him, thrown out of the crowd ... He was tired but he was smiling and he greeted us all with a wave of the hand. He was holding that huge, historic pen with its picture of our Polish Pope on it.

No. 18, female, middle-aged, not working, Olsztyn

Wałęsa becomes a household name

The figure of Lech Wałęsa began to appear in the foreground more and more often.

No. 132, male, student, aged eighteen, Warsaw

Lech Wałęsa's name was being repeated more and more often until eventually it was widely known. On 9 September, when I was coming back from the sanatorium after a course of treatment, the name kept cropping up in conversations at railway stations, in train compartments . . .

No. 74, male, teacher, aged sixty-one

In the mass media the word 'dialogue' and the name 'Wałęsa' are mentioned very frequently together.

No. 104, male, telephone engineer, aged thirty-five, Kutno

Lech Wałęsa and Anna Walentynowicz are on everyone's lips: they are the leaders of the strike.

No. 241, male, stoker, aged fifty-five, Wałbrzych

Workers' impressions

(From a letter sent to the producers of 'Odra', a local radio magazine programme transmitted by Polish Radio, Wrocław)

I think you got carried away a bit when you said that 'In the past we complained about the government, and now we can complain about . . . the church, Wałęsa, etc.' As you are aware, it is common knowledge that Wałęsa stays well away from politics; he cannot, therefore, be accused of trying to rule people. At the same time, Wałęsa knows only too well that there are some people who spend their days loafing about in offices and getting paid the money the workers have to work very hard to provide.

No. 200, female, teacher, aged fifty, Wrocław

My grandad was a union activist – a kind of Wałęsa only on a smaller scale in just one colliery, one mine-shaft – and he used to describe the strikes of the great crisis in 1929.

No. 196, female, Poznań

I shared my impressions with my colleagues at work where I am an electrician, just like Lech Wałęsa.

No. 66, male, electrician, aged thirty-two, Jasień

I treat my pupils very differently now. After Wałęsa, I've grown to respect the working class. I teach with a kind of zeal.

No. 188, female, Elementary Technical School teacher, aged thirty-five, Wrocław

A charismatic leader

Name of Lech Wałęsa, hitherto unknown, he soon turned out to be an extraordinary personality with a forceful character.

No. 214, male, pensioner, aged seventy-eight, Pruszków

L. Wałęsa, a shipyard worker with a moustache, a rosary round his neck and an ostentatious, huge ball-point in his hand. There's something of an uncatholic religious leader about him, something of the prophet. Let's hope he doesn't turn out to be a Polish Khomeini. He speaks simply, spontaneously, and to the point. In a word – he speaks well.

No. 110, male, information specialist, aged forty-nine, Katowice

Every cross in the cemetery at Monte Cassino was adorned by a different rosary – a votive offering left there by nameless visitors. The Chairman of the Strike Committee, Lech Wałęsa, wears a rosary round his neck in much the same way.

No. 184, male, research worker, aged thirty-three

During the first few days, I kept forgetting the strike leader's name. I knew it meant something like 'walk' or 'go'. But later it was to become engraved on my memory forever. A name that is dear to all Poles, to all true Poles: Lech Wałęsa.* I thought to myself: It's no coincidence that his is the most Polish of all their names. Because he is the one who has raised our spirits and he is the one who will get justice for us. He set out on this hard road with God in his heart and that's why he'll reach his goal. He will! If something happened to make me stop believing in him, then my life would lose all meaning. But it won't come to that ... In our home there are five sacred words. They are: God, Poland, bread, and Pope John Paul II and Wałęsa – two heroes of the Polish nation ... Now I felt that I had found myself. I knew the road I had to follow in my life. Like Wałęsa, I would go with God, working for my country and for people, not letting myself, or anyone else, be treated unjustly.

No. 96, female, aged sixteen, Wojnarowo

* '*wałęsa (się)*' means 'loiters' or 'gallivants'.

Voices of dissent

No one seems able to answer the question: 'Who is this leader of the Strike Committee in Gdańsk?' All they can say is that he's called Lech Wałęsa and that he's wringing political concessions out by a calculated aggravation of the problem. Time is working for us. He was probably thrown out of the Party in 1956.

No. 236, male, economist, aged fifty-one, Kraków

In an interview with BBC Radio, Lech Wałęsa said that 'the strikers must win' and that they could keep the strike going for as long as five years. It seems to me that this man isn't aware of the wider context, of Poland's position in Europe. And he doesn't understand that not all the demands can be granted straight away.

No. 178, male, museum director, aged thirty-six,
Nowy Barkoczyn-Będomin

In this exceptionally difficult situation the government is helpless, irresponsible people are intent on seizing power, and even Wałęsa, flaunting his patriotism, can do nothing ... He has to try to maintain his popularity, after all the honours he's received ... But Lech Wałęsa keeps mum because he knows he can't do anything to curb these anarchistic excesses.

No. 214, male, pensioner, aged seventy-eight, Pruszków

August 1980. My husband comes home from work and says that they've been saying in the District Committee that the leader of the strike, Wałęsa, has got a criminal record, is a drunkard and a scrounger. He says that people are confused. They don't know what they're to think of it all.

No. 262, female, pensioner, aged forty-three, Kęty

'They're going on about a renewal, but where is it? It's not that difficult to fathom what Mr Wałęsa's at ... we're the ones who're supposed to be doing the renewing.' Well, that line of argument didn't go down at all well with my colleagues at work. The counter-arguments came thick and fast, and you should have heard them ... 'The man's a buffoon. What's he playing at? Did you see that monstrous pen of his? And what about that rosary? The man's illiterate! Look at the way he sits, leaning on his elbows like that. He's got no respect for the government representatives.

Did you see what he was wearing?' ... I was dumbfounded! ...
No. 240, female, supervisor, aged thirty-four, Poznań

Lech Wałęsa, in the trappings of a workers' leader, goes off to Rome for the Holy Father's blessing, taking his wife and his retinue with him. And it's all paid for out of Solidarity funds or with dollars from America ... Let's hope that when Wałęsa said he'll turn Poland into a second Japan they weren't just empty words. Let's hope we'll restore some order in our country very soon by getting down to work together in peace.

No. 107, male, aged fifty-nine, Opole

Every fool knows why Wałęsa went to the miners: he went to persuade them to come out on strike. He'd do better to stop travelling round all over the place and do some honest work. There's a shortage of electricians in the country. I'd like to know who's paying for the upkeep of his numerous family while he's doing his publicity stunts abroad. One thing's more than certain: there's West German money in all this. He has most certainly improved his material welfare: a nice flat for six people, spending his time putting up monuments, attending meetings, making speeches – if you can call them 'speeches': he wants to learn to read properly. Gentlemen, all this wouldn't be half so disgraceful if you hadn't quite simply over-reached yourselves with that Solidarity of yours. Oh, yes, you've got your Wałęsas and your Bujaks, but you should make very sure that you don't go asking for things that simply cannot be. What you've done to improve things is to ensure that I've got nothing to put on my fire to keep warm, there's nothing in the shops, and everything's much worse than it was before August. [The writer of this account also composed and enclosed a second memoir using the pseudonym 'Gromada' this time. That account was full of dreadful spelling errors. – Marek Latoszek.]

No. 153, male, pseudonym 'Kuszniar' Bartoszyce

Wałęsa at the helm of Solidarity

This is where I recall the words Lech Wałęsa spoke at the official unveiling of the Gdańsk monument. It had taken ten years to get that monument erected, and if it had not been erected then, it would have been put up in the course of one night by people who were committed to the cause.

No. 63, male, economist, aged twenty-five, Bolesławiec

In Gdańsk, the ship 'Solidarity', captained by Lech Wałęsa, has been launched on to the Polish sea ... The brave captain, with Christ at his side, guides the ship through the great storm of strikes and turmoil, through the great crisis in our country, and into the port of a free country ... and so we raise a toast to the captain, Lech Wałęsa, and all the crew of 'Solidarity' – and we wish them all a hundred years of health and good fortune.

No. 228, female, student at a technical college, aged eighteen,
Ruda Śląska

During August a man took his place at the head of his people – a Pole called Lech Wałęsa. The independent trade union Solidarity came into being and assembled in its ranks young and old, everyone who sought the good of our country.

No. 204, male, tiler, aged forty-nine, Warsaw

Warsaw, 30 August 1980

To: Comrade Lech Wałęsa
    The Gdańsk Shipyard
    Gdańsk

I am a former member of the Sejm for the electoral district of Sosnowiec in the period 1935–8. I, and senator Emil Bobrowski from the Kraków electoral district, organized a Parliamentary Labour Group which consisted of members of both chambers (the Sejm and the Senate). This group compiled and published a policy document entitled: 'Proposals Dealing with the Current Problems Facing the World of Labour'. These proposals, known by their working title of 'The Reform of the Social System in Poland', contained, among other things, the basic principles guiding us in the preparation of four statutes which were to be presented before Parliament for legislation. The four statutes concerned were:
(1) a statute dealing with trade unions;
(2) a statute about Works Committees;
(3) a statute relating to a Chamber of Labour;
(4) a statute relating to a Supreme Economic Chamber based on proposals put forward by the world of labour.

The proposed legislation which, as its instigator, I prepared in the name of the Parlimentary Labour Group was to have been presented for debate in the Sejm during its first sitting in the autumn session of 1938. In the meantime, however, as you know, both chambers of Parliament were dissolved prematurely in September 1938. The present demands put forward by the industrial plants led by the Gdańsk shipyard correspond to a large extent to the legislation dealing with the trade unions which we proposed then. It is with a profound and personal interest, therefore, that I have been following the work begun in these last few days by the workers of the Gdańsk shipyard. As the man who had once intended to introduce in Parliament a debate which was to initiate a reform of the social system, I would like to thank you, Comrade Chairman, and all those who have helped you and supported you over these last few days in this Deed of Great Hope, the living symbol of which were all those people who came out on strike. They deserve the gratitude of every single Pole because they have set the Polish truth in motion, they have restored a sense of dignity to a world of labour which is Polish and fully and freely organized. I would like to endorse your work and your words with all my faith, and with my utmost appreciation of your personal contribution. I wish you every success in this labour for good. I believe that the present achievements of the workers will go down into Polish social history, and into the world's chronicles of the struggle for social justice, into the accounts of the dignity of organized labour, as well as the accounts of friendly co-existence between neighbouring nations and their working classes.

I consider it my social duty to draw your attention to the above-mentioned legislative initiatives, particularly at this moment when the task of social renewal lies in your hands and in the hands of your comrades.

I am, with all respect to you, Comrade Chairman, and the work-force of the Gdańsk shipyard,

No. 91, Zbigniew Madejski, pre-war Member of Parliament,
aged eighty-three, Warsaw

P.S. Some traces of the documents appertaining to the above-mentioned legislative initiatives can be found in the Library of the Sejm. (See also: A. Ajenkiel, Institute of History at the Polish Academy of Sciences, paper dated 30 April 1975.)

Then a new union organization came into being. It's called the independent trade union 'Solidarity' and is led by its magnificent leader – Lech Wałęsa.

No. 90, male, economist, aged fifty-two, Warsaw

All of us Poles of good faith should work hard and keep that green light burning in this country of ours, just as the leader of the independent trade union Solidarity, Lech Wałęsa, has urged us to do so many times.

No. 32, male, Włocławek

These memoirs go to make up a piece of retrospective documentation, since some of them were written only after the events of August 1980. The amount of time that has elapsed since then, however, is not enough to have allowed subsequent experiences to distort the general response to those events to any great extent. Consequently, the accounts which we received retain, in full, a freshness of reaction to those events. The interesting thing is that it has been possible to construct a fairly detailed portrait of Wałęsa just by using quotations taken from a much larger context. Facts from his life, his personal characteristics, his idiosyncrasies, his manner – all these have emerged from the memoirs. Because he is the focal point for people's attention, Wałęsa does tend to be idealized. But he is also slandered, even if those slanders do arise from misconceptions and gossip. It should be underlined that people were writing about him within the context of the events of August 1980. Their attitudes towards those events went a long way in shaping their attitudes to Wałęsa himself. It should also be borne in mind that he appears in two different roles. The first is that of the leader of the strike, the second is that of chairman of the independent trade union Solidarity. These roles provoke somewhat different evaluations, made on quite different bases.

Compiled and selected by Marek Latoszek

Chapter 10

'*I Am Indebted for It to This Man with a Moustache*'

An Interview with Andrzej Wajdą by Maria Mrozińska

MARIA MROZIŃSKA: Talking about John Paul II's visit to Poland, Professor Bogdan Suchodolski observed that the work of scholars, scientists and artists who think they have something important to tell their countrymen does not seem to have much effect. And suddenly a man appears who all at once is able to draw millions of people to himself. This is also true of the phenomenon of Wałęsa. What do you think about it?

ANDRZEJ WAJDĄ: I wouldn't agree with Professor Suchodolski. For a man like Wałęsa to appear on the horizon of our political life, our work had been necessary. Professor Suchodolski had worked for it, I had worked for it, and so had very many people in Poland, those who deal with the arts and with formulating views. It may be that our work does not seem very impressive and next to the dazzling phenomenon of Wałęsa somehow disappears. Still, our ambitions do not consist of showing off. Our ambitions ought to be placed in expectation. We, the intellectuals and artists of today, have been very lucky, because we can say that something has resulted from our work.

MARIA MROZIŃSKA: In an interview for *Polityka* you have said that you feel the need for a more direct action; for stepping beyond the forms in which you have expressed yourself up to now. Does not this correspond in some degree to Professor Suchodolski's difficult reflection on the work of artists and intellectuals?

ANDRZEJ WAJDĄ: The need for direct action results above all from the fact that possibilities for such action now exist. Up to now, when we expressed ourselves through film, through word, through thought, there were no other possibilities. Today I think that the existence of a huge trade union, with ten million members, gives the chance to speak and act directly.

MARIA MROZIŃSKA: Wałęsa is the leader of that union. He emerged because he had articulated the ideas dormant in society, and the great idea of Solidarity was born.

ANDRZEJ WAJDA: Maybe even not so much ideas as expectations and hopes.

MARIA MROZIŃSKA: To what extent is the phenomenon of Wałęsa the result of his having voiced these expectations and hopes, and how much is it the effect of his personality?

ANDRZEJ WAJDA: One is connected with the other. They are not two separate elements. He had responded to those expectations and said what everyone wanted to hear, because he had the courage to say it out loud, and in such a simple way. This was astounding to all of us, who had been used to speeches of politicians, speeches based on insinuations, on total camouflage. It has always been like that – it is something recognized in politics. A politician is a man who hides his intentions, his genuine views, so that he can win. Wałęsa's strength in August 1980 consisted in his speaking plainly. Why did he talk openly? Because he understood that his strength did not come from him alone, but from millions of people who think the same as he does only do not speak out. They want to hear things said clearly, undisguised, directly. So when they heard Wałęsa, they said: Yes, he is the man who speaks on our behalf. And only then Wałęsa became who he is now – the exponent of social desires and expectations.

MARIA MROZIŃSKA: In that case one could say he became who he is by accident, that someone else could have emerged just as well. That's why I asked about his personal characteristics.

ANDRZEJ WAJDA: It is possible that someone else from among those who took part in the strike could have articulated those expectations, those social views. I think that those who took part in these events and are now describing them have a feeling that the leader had in a sense emerged by chance. But still there must have been something in Wałęsa's personality which predestined him for leadership. What could it be? When I observe him, it seems to me that he has all the qualities which we Poles treasure. Firstly, he is a courageous man and had proved his courage even earlier, before the August strike. And so he was ready. Secondly, he is a truthful man, who considers telling the truth and saying what he thinks as something natural. Thirdly, he has a sense of humour, something that in the case of politicians who have not been nominated or elected but appear the way Wałęsa has done is a matter of decisive importance. Wałęsa has a sense of humour both with regard to himself and to the situation in which he finds himself. That enables him to behave in the right way in surprising and unforeseeable situations. I listened very attentively to all the speeches he uttered by the shipyard gate, because I wanted to use one of them as the final sequence of my film. Listening to these speeches I noticed that he was accepted by all the people standing by that gate. It seems to me that the three elements I have mentioned are decisive here.

MARIA MROZIŃSKA: He is charged with a lack of organizing abilities, and this is considered to disqualify him as a leader. They say that to carry crowds with him, which he does very well, is definitely not enough.

ANDRZEJ WAJDA: Perhaps, though it has to be said that there are many people who are good organizers, but few have the three qualities I have mentioned. And if Wałęsa really does not possess the capacity to organize, it only needs to be asked if he can find good administrators who would translate his intentions into everyday practice; those who by their unflagging efforts would carry into effect the ideas and concepts which stem from him.

MARIA MROZIŃSKA: Do you think that the future of Solidarity is somehow connected with the question of leadership?

ANDRZEJ WAJDA: Yes and no. What does the strength of that movement consist of? It is like the phoenix rising from ashes, which is cut into pieces and reborn in another place. Many of the Solidarity leaders whom the movement produced after August 1980 are people whom we know well and appreciate today. But we know also that every one of them can be replaced by another. Do you

know why I think that? When I went to the Gdańsk shipyard
during the strike and later went through a mass of material working
on *Man of Iron*, I became curious about one thing: journalists
constantly interviewed people outside the hall where talks were
taking place. Why? It was a result of the most significant idea
of the strike organizers: setting up loudspeakers all over the shipyard. Incidentally, that was not an idea of Wałęsa's or of the praesidium of the Gdańsk Interworks Strike Committee. In 1970 I had
intended to make a film about the events in Szczecin and made
some preparations for it. There was no chance, of course, of such
a film being started, let alone made. Well, I found that at the
Szczecin shipyard the same idea had been used. In view of the lies
people are used to, loudspeakers are very important when the
general principle has been accepted that a group of people should
meet in seclusion and agree on decisions that would be binding
for everybody. Secrecy was unacceptable to the strikers, who
gathered here of their own free will. Everyone wanted to know
how far the talks had got. The loudspeakers enabled every striker
to be as aware of what was happening as the leadership was. One
day's leader could be replaced by others the next day, because
all the people outside the hall gave the journalists interviewing
them exactly the same answers as Wałęsa gave to the Deputy Prime
Minister, Jagielski. What does this mean? It means that here was
not a case to be fought by a few leaders on behalf of all the other
workers. The leaders were only articulating more clearly the awareness shared by all. The striking workers *en masse* not only had
that awareness, but were also able to articulate it, and that was,
and is, the strength of the movement. In place of every leader,
including Wałęsa, someone else will be found. That means they
are indestructible. This indestructibility consists of the awareness
of the working class. It is not just a matter of who has the greater
personality. Wałęsa certainly has a marvellous personality and that
is why he was declared the Man of the Year for 1980. He also
has an engaging personality. But I am deeply convinced that if
one day he were no longer with us, in his place would come someone
equally mature, equally serious, with the same views and with the
aims which Wałęsa is endeavouring to reach. This is the thing
that gives me the greatest optimism as far as the Solidarity movement is concerned.

MARIA MROZIŃSKA: In March 1981, as you know, some members of the National Co-ordinating Committee of Solidarity put forward charges that Wałęsa had attempted to establish something like a conspiracy of leaders, that is to say that he had conducted negotiations in a closed group, without contacting the rest of the committee. This caused a debate on democracy in the movement.

ANDRZEJ WAJDA: One has to begin with what democracy is. Democracy means also that the minority has the right to speak, but in Poland up to now democracy has meant exclusively the right of majority. In the period now ended the masses had no say at all, while individuals usurped the right to speak on their behalf. Because of that, we were saying: This is not democracy, the masses must have their say. And they have now. But true democracy will be brought about when individuals have their say. Solidarity is on the way to true democracy. All this is still ahead of us. The democratic system does not have a long history in Poland. Every now and then a chance for democracy appears. Poles begin to think democratically, try to create institutions which would guarantee democracy, and then the political situation forces these institutions to be disbanded and everything returns to its former state. Just now the student movement, if one looks at it closely, shows very clearly how little people are prepared for democracy, how they do not understand it at all. For that reason, to find out if Wałęsa fights using right or wrong methods one has to talk about the general concept of democracy. One must remember also for whom he fights, on whose behalf, and then assess what he must or must not do. It is certainly fine and good that the entire union is on its guard against the infringement of the idea of democracy, the idea of free choice. At present, democracy functions on behalf of the majority, but it will flourish fully only when all those who hold views different from those generally accepted will not have to suffer for them.

MARIA MROZIŃSKA: They say about Wałęsa that he represents the ethics of responsibility, not the ethics of intention; that in his actions he is motivated above all by a sense of responsibility as the highest moral precept, and less by an intention to maintain full democracy in the union. In other words, he is a pragmatist.

ANDRZEJ WAJDĄ: I agree. Wałęsa is a pragmatist, and I think this is good for our cause. A man in his position should be pragmatic. Alas, Poles often fight for imponderables rather than for essentials. I have the impression that Wałęsa fights for the essence of things; he makes concessions where he ought to and does not make them where he should not. There will always be people who think that his concessions concern essentials, but this is the fate of every politician. Wałęsa must realize that, having entered this path, he has to submit to criticism and that criticism will be more severe because the expectations are greater. This is the kind of situation where his sense of humour may help him. Outlining his profile I have, perhaps, left out one thing. The Polish image of a worker is quite different from the reality. For instance, when I met him for the first time, with no idea that such a man existed – before my arrival at the shipyard on 30 August I had been very badly informed – and I looked at him, my first impression was that he would best fit the part of Pan Wołodyjowski.*

MARIA MROZIŃSKA: They call him the 'little knight' ...

ANDRZEJ WAJDĄ: That was exactly what I thought ... with his moustache, his sense of humour, sometimes even his melancholy ... he is the 'little knight'. He is not a product of working-class culture, which, as they wanted us to believe, is supposedly quite different. Wałęsa is the product of Polish culture. For such a man to emerge and reap such a harvest, cultural traditions were essential. For instance, there had to be a Sienkiewicz to write his trilogy; then there had to be those who, in the blackest period of Stalinist repression, decided it was a book which must not disappear but must be re-published – there had been attempts to suppress it. All this helped to shape the awareness of our national identity. Wałęsa has grown out of this awareness, this tradition, this profoundly Polish way of thinking. Someone may ask me whether it would not be better if the leader of such a big trade union were an unemotional, sober man who knew everything, had thought everything over and who in a critical moment would emerge victorious from the fight. One can wonder if someone

* See footnote on p. 132.

like that would not be better for our movement. Maybe he would. If ever a moment comes when Solidarity recognizes that such a man is necessary, there is nothing to prevent him from assuming leadership. Very few people have been made for all seasons. Each of us knows from his own experience in life that there are moments when he proves himself, and others when he is useless. At any rate, one thing is certain with regard to Wałęsa: today we cannot imagine that anyone else but him could accomplish what was done in August 1980.

Bearing in mind the many years of official cultural activity aimed at dividing people from each other, there ought to exist an artificially created working-class culture and – quite separately – a culture of the intelligentsia (which is really the lineal descendant of the culture of the pld petty nobility). Those attempts resulted in awakening the ambitions of the working class, but did not succeed in pushing it in the direction desired by the manipulators. The workers were somehow drawn into the sphere of culture represented by the intelligentsia. And this is a great, a marvellous victory. Wałęsa does not have to say that he has read books, seen films, been interested in discussions. This is not important. What matters is that somehow all this got through to him and that he is a representative of that particular line and no other. And, of course, he could be an exponent of a quite different line, much more orthodox and much less Polish and national.

MARIA MROZIŃSKA: Talking in an interview about *Man of Iron*, you said that the film in a sense transgresses against the art of film, because the emphasis is on words. This is because what Wałęsa actually says is more important than his visual appearance, say, at the shipyard gate. This statement of yours means that you are looking to the future, to the ideas whose realization can give Solidarity a greater strength, and also consolidate all the important changes in the people and in the country. What do you consider most important for the future of that post-strike message, the words that were uttered, the events that occurred?

ANDRZEJ WAJDA: It seems to me that the most important was the fact that the workers used symbols which had been reserved for the authorities. The workers put out the white-and-red flag, displayed the crowned Eagle, and later sawed the crown off.* I see in the use of these symbols a feeling of responsibility on the part of the workers for the country as a whole, not only for themselves. And yet, after thirty-five years, they could have felt, and would have had the right to feel, responsible only for themselves, turn their backs on everything and say: those are not our interests. It is also most important that the workers raised subjects like censorship and spoke up for the Church. After all, they did not have to do it.

MARIA MROZIŃSKA: You arrived at Gdańsk shipyard on 29 August. Why did you go?

ANDRZEJ WAJDA: I have already mentioned my intention to make a film about the events of 1970 in Szczecin and my being thwarted in this. I took it badly at the time, and now I knew I must not let the chance slip, I must be ready. I knew that this was an event I had to see with my own eyes. There had been such different, contradictory opinions. The visit to the shipyard changed me completely. I went there thinking that things had been strained to their utmost limits and that the strikers needed to strive urgently for an agreement. I saw the situation as analogous to the course of a performance, where up to a certain point there is tension, and beyond it – a fall, whether one wants it or not. This is something independent of the rightness, the justice of the cause, such is the law of performance. It seemed to me that this show had already reached its culmination and that now there would be a sudden fall. I was afraid of a situation where there would be workers on strike, somewhere at the Gdańsk shipyard, but the media, the people, all would turn away from them, asking: What is the matter? What do they want? That's how I viewed the situation when I was on my way to the Gdańsk shipyard. After a talk with Wałęsa, I left it as an entirely different man. I realized that my previous reasoning had been hopelessly petty; it had been the reasoning of a man who did not understand what was at stake.

*The crowned (Royal) Eagle had been the national emblem of Poland. The communist regime, established after the Second World-War, retained the Eagle as the emblem of People's Poland but removed the crown.

Wałęsa said to me: Mr Wajda, this may be the last chance for our country. I understood then that this matter could not be considered in the way I had done before; that it must be considered in the context of our national existence, not of the victory of the Gdańsk shipyard over provincial and central authority. I suddenly realized that Wałęsa had in himself a much greater sense of historic responsibility, historic importance, than I had. I was impressed by this. No matter what happens to him in future, no matter how the voters assess him, the fact will remain that at a time when nobody had yet thought this was an event of world importance, it was he who gave it that status and imparted it to all those whom he met.

MARIA MROZIŃSKA: How do you think he came to the conviction that this was the last chance for Poland?

ANDRZEJ WAJDA: I think there were two reasons for this. One was the crime committed in December 1970. A very strong reason. Everywhere in the world police shoot at demonstrators, people die, but how different this looks in a country which calls itself a working people's country. One cannot with impunity shoot at workers in a working people's country, as this is totally incompatible not only with ideology but with the most elementary sense of justice. And yet it happened. This is the first cause: Wałęsa speaks with the voice of the dead. The second is his working-class ideology. It is something quite incomprehensible in the West, when he is shown with a picture of the Madonna and a rosary. When the great Spanish film director Buñuel had seen Wałęsa with a rosary on television, he said to his screen writer, with whom he is now working and who had written for him scenarios of such well-known films as *The Discreet Charm of the Bourgeoisie* and *Diary of a Chambermaid*: No, this is improbable. How can a workers' leader be religious? This is a contradiction in itself. And yet Wałęsa, the religious Wałęsa, does not cease to be a man who thinks in materialist terms; he speaks for the rights of the working class on whose behalf Marx wrote and acted.

MARIA MROZIŃSKA: While you were at Gdańsk shipyard, you gave an interview for the strike bulletin *Solidarity*. You said there: 'I have always thought I could do a sequel to that film' (*Man of*

Marble). Did you have a vision of this film, the continued story of your hero, even before August 1980?

ANDRZEJ WAJDĄ: The continued story of my hero had to be inseparably bound up with the Polish reality, and I did not, could not, imagine how it would develop; I could not foresee events that were to happen. I was not alone in this. I think that nobody in Poland could foresee them. Maybe that is why some Polish intellectuals are against what happened, for the sole reason that they did not invent, did not foresee it.

MARIA MROZIŃSKA: But were you thinking of making a film sequel?

ANDRZEJ WAJDĄ: I very much wanted to do it and that was why in the last sequence of *Man of Marble* that couple appeared walking down the corridor: Janda and Radziwiłłowicz – they walked towards a future. But how that future was to look, I did not know. I only knew that one day something had to change, that things could not go on as they were.

MARIA MROZIŃSKA: So the vision of *Man of Iron* was really born in August 1980?

ANDRZEJ WAJDĄ: It was born first of the hope that changes were inevitable, but the real substance materialized only during those August days. Not only the substance, but its possibilities. The official reception of *Man of Marble* had been such that I did not have the slightest chance even to touch on that subject. August opened up two possibilities. Firstly, I knew now what would be the subject of the film. Secondly, it enabled me to make the film at all.

MARIA MROZIŃSKA: A review published after the Cannes Festival in the French newspaper *France Soir* said that the award for acting should have been given to Lech Wałęsa as the prototype of the hero of *Man of Iron*. But the story of the film hero is quite remote from Wałęsa's life history.

ANDRZEJ WAJDĄ: I could not produce a story with Lech Wałęsa as the hero for the simple reason that I wanted him to take part in the film. It is the first film of this kind, but I do not think that the subject is exhausted in it or that it shows the August events in the most proper way. It had happened several times in my life that my films were made just when they were expected, so I thought I should do the same this time too. I think that is my role in all this. However, I do not think that I have succeeded in doing everything the way I wanted to do. We do not have the full picture and knowledge of the origins of August events as yet. Many elements are hard to grasp and I excluded them from my film.

MARIA MROZIŃSKA: Czesław Miłosz said at a recent meeting with shipyard workers, at whose invitation he was visiting Gdańsk: 'What I feel for Lech Wałęsa and the shipyard workers can be expressed in one word – gratitude.'

ANDRZEJ WAJDĄ: He put it well. Coming from him this sounds stronger and more beautiful, for the changes in Poland do not concern him directly. My gratitude, on the other hand, has more direct causes. Thanks to what had happened, I could do the film I wanted to do; thanks to these events I can think with hope about many matters concerning cinema and culture in general. It is important today that one should not wait for global changes in the central system. The system will be transformed very slowly. I, for instance, am not waiting for the re-organization of cinematography, but am making films. At the same time, within my means, I do what I can to bring about that re-organization. But I do not wait for it to happen first, so that I can then set about making films. Even within the limits of existing 'impossibility' one has to do what is possible. Otherwise, in spite of our wonderful ideology, we shall have to give ourselves into the hands of other people, because we shall have no influence on reality any more. That's why I like Wałęsa's programme and action; for it is the action of a man who knows reality, searches for agreement, for a way out, because extreme solutions are unacceptable.

MARIA MROZIŃSKA: You spoke about the great impression that Wałęsa's words 'this may be the last chance' made on you. This finds its expression in the last scene of *Man of Iron*, when Maciek Tomczyk says that now we will never let ourselves be divided, we will always go together towards the future, a difficult future maybe, but together. In these words there is an assertion that this was the last chance, but there is also hope.

ANDRZEJ WAJDĄ: Yes, August 1980 influenced very seriously my way of looking at the Polish reality: I saw that hope. This is stated in the film. We have seen truth and now nobody will be able to deny he has seen it. This is the most important fact. For having seen that truth I am indebted to this man with a moustache, whom I did not know before, whose existence I had not suspected, and who expresses the desires and expectations of millions of people.

Chapter 11

Wałęsa – an Action Portrait

(Lech Wałęsa interviewed by Marzena and Tadeusz Woźniak)

'I'll give you seven minutes. Fire away ...'

'We're not doing a press interview. We'd like you to give us two hours.'

'Out of the question. What's it for?'

'There's a book being published. The first book about Wałęsa in this country. So we don't want to do just a superficial interview.'

'I'm not interested in books. When I have a bit more time, I'll write one myself. Why should you be the ones who make money out of it, not me? Anyway, times are hard now and people should be getting down to some real work. I advise you to do the same. You can have seven minutes or nothing at all.'

'We've lost three minutes arguing – will they come off the seven you've given us?'

'We'll just have to wait and see, won't we. Fire away ...'

'You won't be evasive in your answers, will you?'

'I always give straight answers to people's questions. I have nothing to hide.'

'In other words you see yourself as sincere, honest and frank, do you?'

'That's right.'

'Would you say that those were desirable qualities in the field of politics?'

'What I meant was ... Look, obviously you can't say everything there is to say. And even though I can and do answer every question put to me, I can't be expected to reveal every single detail.'

'So you are a tactician, are you?'

'If someone tries to lead me up the garden path, then I pay him back with a bit of the same. There's a little bit of game-playing involved, you know.'

'Only a little? Or is there quite a lot?'

'Yes, you're right. Sometimes there is quite a lot. It's like playing for very high stakes. Sometimes. But I'm a good player.'

'What tactics do you use with your own people – the people from Solidarity? I mean, it's no secret that the union is far from being a monolithic organization and that you've been forced to fight your corner even there.'

'Of course there are differences of opinion. There are people, for example, who want to see as many agreements as possible signed. Others would prefer to concentrate on getting what's been signed already put into practice. Personally, I'm one of those who want to put things into practice. I'm not interested in signing more agreements.'

'Are there any people in the union you can be a hundred per cent sure of?'

'No, there aren't. I can't be a hundred per cent sure of myself, come to that.'

'You make it sound as if you sensed you were alone ...'

'That's quite true. I've always been alone, I'm alone now and I probably always will be alone.'

'Have you never experienced again that sense of community that was present in August?'

'That feeling can only happen at a huge mass meeting. When there are a lot of people – for example, in Wrocław there were a hundred thousand people. There was an atmosphere of total understanding there. Well, I can always generate that kind of situation, of course.'

'Hang on a minute. Do you really generate the situation – or is it the crowd that does it?'

'I influence it. There's no doubt about that.'

'How exactly do you do it? How do you get a crowd of a hundred thousand people ready to go through fire for you?'

'By getting through to them. If I'm given enough time to find out what concerns people have got, then I'll get through to them. Doesn't matter if they live in the East or the West. That's what happened in Japan. We made no headway in the first three days.

Every time someone got up to speak to the people, he lost them. Bujak and Rulewski both got nowhere. Couldn't get any kind of communication going. They weren't Japanese, you see. We needed three days of asking questions, finding things out and then, after three days, I felt that I was Japanese. I could go out to them and share their truths with them. I said to them: You spend your evenings counting your money, you fiddle people, you're well fed, of course, but does that mean that you're happy? I asked them if all they needed for happiness was bread and sausage. I asked them: What do you want out of life? What is the purpose of your lives? They don't believe in God – that's their business. But they must believe in love, in their children, or even in their wretched money. Man has got to believe in something. If he doesn't, he becomes an animal. A dangerous animal.'

'You've got your faith, and you've got your purpose in life worked out. Are you happy?'

'I never have been happy, and I don't know that I ever will be. I take your point. It's much easier to spout theory. Nevertheless, nowadays people prefer to spout theories and get involved in discussions about happiness rather than get into technological progress.'

'Do you see yourself as irreplaceable in your present role?'

'Far from it. I am replaceable. Furthermore, in order to safe-guard the union's future, I want all the important decisions to be taken not in small enclaves but by a large cross-section of society. So I'm going to try to limit the powers of individuals to make decisions which affect the country as a whole.'

'Very well. You say you're not irreplaceable. But how do you see yourself – as a real leader, or more as a symbol?'

'Symbol indeed! What a thing to say! You know very well that I have no wish to be any kind of symbol.'

'How much of the decision-making process is in your hands? What specifically needs your participation?'

'Almost everything does. Especially the very crucial questions. Nobody is prepared to make decisions without me.'

'Do you always know what you have to do? How do you come to your decisions?'

'It takes seconds. Split seconds. Those are the best decisions. The ones you make in a split second are best. Those that are weighed up, chewed over, compromised on – they're no good.'

'How often do your views conflict with the views of the majority? And what happens then?'

'It does happen, of course. It happened in Bydgoszcz when they wanted an immediate strike. I walked out of the hall and gave them eight hours to reconsider. They did and they agreed that I was right, and the meeting was wrong.'

'Are there other ways of getting what you want?'

'Of course there are. It all depends on how much time there is and on the options available.'

'In that case, can you really say there's any democracy within Solidarity?'

'When I say "democracy" I don't mean the gaggling of geese.'

'What is democracy, then, since you seem to find it so irritating at times? To what extent is it useful in your activities?'

'There haven't been any important decisions made undemocratically – and I'm not talking about the gaggling democracy, either. We made a very serious mistake at the very beginning. We should have gone out and educated the people. We should have explained things to them, got them to reach a certain common level of thought. We didn't do it, and it's costing us dear now. Oh, yes, we've come a long way in that we talk about democracy. But the levels of thought we bring to bear on the subject are very variable indeed. And it's proving a great obstacle at our meetings, during discussions, in the decision-making process and so on. It makes us all very vulnerable. We can be manipulated in all sorts of ways. Not to put too fine a point on it – we're not properly disciplined.'

'And is that why you sometimes have to bang your fist on the table?'

'That's right.'

'Can you be quite sure of your decisions? How can you be so confident?'

'Because I've thought my ideas through thoroughly.'

'Yes, but what has shaped them? What is their cornerstone?'

'My whole life. I've been able to take note, listen and watch ever since I was a child – I've always spied on life. I think I've come to know it a little.'

'Do you want to influence the course of history, and the fate of this country?'

'Yes and no.'

'That's not an answer. Do you know what you want? Do you know where you're leading millions of people? Are you following a specific vision, a shape of the future?'

'This is neither the time nor the place to go into all that. Its realization depends on so many serious factors that I'm profoundly concerned about it. I know very well what I want. I have a vision and I'm capable of putting a lot of things right. I can bring about the kind of Poland we would all like to see. I'm quite capable of manoeuvring my way through and capturing the prize. But to do that I'd have to stop dissipating my energy on unnecessary and stupid in-fighting at plenary meetings and at praesidium meetings.'

'Should anything go wrong – which, pray God, it won't – but if it does, would you be prepared to take the responsibility entirely on your own shoulders? Or will you share it with others – democratically?'

'No, I'm prepared to take all the blame myself. Having said that, though, I know that if it was a question of making that bleakest and most difficult of decisions, then I wouldn't take it myself, off my own bat. Instead of that I'd go to the people and I'd say: Look, the risk is enormous. If we go on, we'll lose. If you want to go on, I'll go with you – but we'll have to share the responsibility. I can expose myself to danger – that's my business. But I would never take a decision that would put society as a whole at risk on my own. That's why, if it began to look as if things might turn into a great gamble, then I'd settle the question of responsibility once and for all. Before we took the plunge. The responsibility will be joint. Assuming, of course, that I'm in the country and that I have enough time to say anything at all.'

'In Bydgoszcz, you got the impression that the views of the majority weren't being fairly reflected in the hall. Is that right?'

'Yes. The same thing happened in Warsaw. But you must understand that there was more to it than that. Sometimes, someone gets things wrong – these things happen ... Let's not go into whether Bydgoszcz was right or not just now. What really happened was that we were in danger of splitting up; splitting away from the Church especially. And at times like that you've got to turn back. We must not allow ourselves to be fragmented. Even if the price we have to pay is to take a step back. The main thing was to stay united at a moment of extreme danger. I realized that we couldn't allow discord to creep in, that we had to stick together. But these are all behind-the-scene machinations which will be brought to light by future generations.'

'Do you, a man who is "creating history", necessarily need to understand history? What I mean is, did you always, at any given moment, have a clear grasp of every situation as it was in the process of developing?'

'I tried to, though we haven't got the necessary back-up information to give us a full picture. But I do try to know about as many things as I can so I can see how they fall into place at a given moment, and how they might fall into place in the future.'

'A question especially for Lech Wałęsa: To what extent did the events of August 1980 come as a surprise to you?'

'They didn't. Though, actually ... Let's go back to the beginning. Before August 1980 we, in the opposition, often discussed the possibilities of calling a strike and when it could be done. I was one of those who wanted to postpone things. What I mean is that I needed another year. If it had all happened a year later instead of in August 1980 then we might have avoided a lot of the problems we're having to cope with right now. Because up until it all happened, I had everything – the whole thing – thought out and worked out. When I say "worked out" I don't mean that I had a detailed plan of action. All I mean is that I had it sorted out in my own self. I was fully convinced of where we had to go, why, how, and so on. What happened, though, was that, after the strike, things became very volatile. Now I have to respond from minute to minute to things which are developing continuously, I have to improvise, and, at the same time as I'm doing all that, I'm having to convince myself of the correctness of a course of action. So that it's consistent, you see, so that what I say and what I think and believe are more or less in concert. And that's proving to be a great drain on my energy and my health. The thing is you can't indulge in any sleight-of-hand. All that twisting and turning, all that trickery and jiggery-pokery – all that's no good. You have to have an inner conviction that a course of action is the right course and then everything will go smoothly. Just like it's been going so far. The future is a bit uncomfortable inasmuch as I've got to put it in some kind of order from day to day and then convert myself to it.'

'Don't you get the impression that you've bitten off more than you can chew? That you've been overtaken by history?'

'No, no, no! I've got things sorted out inside far enough ahead now. I really do have a vision about what I'm doing now, I do know what needs to be done, and how to do it. It's just that I'm short of strength ...'

'In other words, the question of whether it's you who's in command of the situation, or the situation which is in charge of you, is not valid.'

'That's right. It's not valid.'

'All right, then – try jumping out of this careering train and returning to the shipyard as an ordinary worker.'

'Well, of course, that isn't possible. There have been times since August 1980 when I've wanted to resign from the leadership. I'd like to give it up now. But before I can do that I must make sure that everything is under control and moving along on the right tracks. Afterwards, I'll still want to have my say, but not standing in the spotlight like now.'

'You've become public property ...'

'You mean a slave, don't you? I haven't got a life. I'm not living at all.'

'What does history look like to somebody on the inside? Is it logical? Does it have some sense?'

'Not always. Not always. If people could only hear those snatches of conversations, see those bits of skulduggery with people trying to pull the wool over each other's eyes ... Jagielski trying it on me. Me trying it on Jagielski ... At the moment you can't reveal any of that, but sometime people will be told all about it, they'll be shown how that stew is prepared in history's kitchen.'

'Are there things which are historically impossible? People say that August 1980 was a miracle.'

'I wouldn't put too much store by miracles like that. Though we were extraordinarily lucky, I do admit that. Every time we fired, we hit the bull. It was as if the bulls'-eyes were coming out to meet the bullets. Added to that there was an unbelievable series of external coincidences. You know the Polish saying about man doing the shooting and God carrying the bullets. From time to time I analyse some of the decisions I made off the cuff. Even professors have analysed them, and they can't explain why they worked,

either. They can't say anything about them at all: they were very
ordinary decisions. Except that they were the best ones that could
have been made at a given moment. A lot of things have turned out
in such a way that now, no matter how hard you tried to work them
out, you simply couldn't come up with the same answers and the
same situations again.'

'In private conversations people keep asking questions like:
"Who was 'behind' the happenings in August? Who got the whole
thing 'on the road'?" Was it a spontaneous movement, or was it
a carefully orchestrated thing by conspirators who were out to seize
power?'

'I can't speak for those at the top. I've already told you that for
me, personally, August was very inconvenient. I wanted to put the
brakes on. After all, we weren't ready. There were no plans for
afterwards. But, at the same time, we knew that if the social
situation had come to a head we couldn't stand aside. We had to
get involved. We wouldn't waste opportunities like they were
wasted in 1956 and 1970. And that's the preparedness, that's the
preliminary preparation that was in evidence during the strike. But
there was no "orchestration" from me. There was no score. The
best proof of that is that the strike kept collapsing every five
minutes. I must have gone down to various sections at least five
times, leading them in song, just to pick up the pieces again. There
was no manual of instructions telling me what I had to do and how.'

'What's the real story about you giving up the strike on the
third day?'

'All that's been written about that so far is sheer nonsense. I
mean, is it really so hard to figure out that it was just a tactical
ploy? Look, the first strike committee in the shipyard was just
young kids. There came a moment when I realized that there was a
revolution being prepared, that there was another committee
starting up, a committee consisting of older men. More staid
people. So, straight away, I issued a recommendation that our
committee be increased in size, that we take in three people from
each section, and that they would be older workers. Naturally
enough, the committee started to fill up with people who were
manipulated. I started to lose in the votes, things started to crack
up. I thought – what can I do? I mean, I couldn't just kick those
people off the committee, could I? So then, without consulting

anyone about my decision, I agreed to support the move to wind up the strike. But I knew in advance that it was just a sham, that it was a ploy I had to make to get rid of those uncertain elements, those people who had been set up. If I could get them to run away from the strike, we would have smashed the second line and cleaned out the committee. And I would continue the struggle at the head of those who remained in the shipyard. I knew that a hundred people would stay inside for sure, and I would lead them in a strike of solidarity. I was a bit anxious about Sunday, of course. I was afraid we might be moved out once we were left on our own. But I took the chance. I tell you, I'd rather have a hundred, or even twenty, really hard men by my side than thousands of uncertain people. That's the way it happened. It was like playing a hand at poker: I cleaned out the committee and strengthened my own position at the same time. And yet, for some reason, it looks as if no one is prepared to accept it. In fact, they reproach me for giving the strike up too soon, and they say that someone else had to step in and save it.'

'Are you saying that you feel that people haven't been giving you your due? Even though they carry you on their shoulders at rallies?'

'People have forgotten about a lot of the things that happened at the very beginning, things that were decisive in shaping the entire social movement after August. Take, for example, the question of involving the academics in the strike. Today, people are saying that Solidarity is a veritable model of the alliance between the workers and the intelligentsia. A model which can teach the rest of the world. But nobody cares to remember how I was reviled for getting the academics and the writers involved in the strike. In August, I was accused of acting like a dictator because I co-opted Bądkowski and Gruszewski on to the praesidium.* The fact is that as soon as they arrived with their declarations of support I decided, despite opposition, that they should be on the praesidium. I had to do that because I wanted to have as many social groups as possible represented. And what did some of the others say? No, let me refresh your memories. They said that we should send all those

---

*Lech Bądkowski, a novelist from the Gdańsk area, and Wojciech Gruszewski, a lecturer in chemical engineering at Gdańsk Polytechnic, were among the signatories of the Gdańsk agreement of 31 August 1980.

intellectuals to the devil, that we would be able to manage on our own, and that we would show them just how much we can do without anyone's help. That's the way it was, but nobody's particularly keen to bring it to light. Instead of which they're all going on about the unity of the movement, about there not being any isolated groups and so on.'

'Come, come, there was more to it than just a nicely played poker hand ... It does seem that you've got that rare intuitive gift of knowing which alternative to choose. That could well prove more valuable than a fully prepared programme.'

'Why do you keep getting at me about this programme? If I tell you I've got a programme, then I have. But a good player doesn't slap all his cards on the table straight off, does he? And I've got a whole mass of cards that haven't been played yet.'

'Why do you keep using analogies with games of chance? Can't political activity be described in some other way?'

'We should all be pleased that it's only a game still.'

'Do you understand the government people better than you did before?'

'Without a doubt, yes. All that that means, though, is that I trust them even less.'

'Doesn't that understanding pose a bit of a threat to Solidarity? What I mean is, can you guarantee that you will always be aware of what and whom you represent?'

'Of course I can. When there's a problem that needs solving, then I don't care what the man's name or position is. It doesn't matter who is sitting opposite me. The important thing is to be able to outwit him, divert him, and grab what there is to be won. I don't look to see if it's Rakowski or Jaruzelski.* We sit down at a table, I put forward my proposal, he comes up with a counter-proposal. We interrupt one another, the temperature rises, I get up, bang my fist on the table – and then I leave. It's happened so many times ... I walked out on the Prime Minister without so much as a word.

* Mieczysław Rakowski, an editor, was appointed a Deputy Prime Minister in early 1981 and was Wałęsa's main negotiating opponent for the rest of the year. General Wojciech Jaruzelski, Minister of Defence since 1968, was appointed Prime Minister in February 1981. In October he was elected First Secretary of the Polish United Workers' Party in addition to his other offices. On 13 December 1981, Jaruzelski carried out a military *coup d'état* which crushed Solidarity and deprived Lech Wałęsa – with many thousands of his colleagues – of his liberty.

The same thing happened at Kania's.* When I'm after some sort of settlement they're all just opponents, even if, privately, I quite like some of them. That's the way it is ... But if I'm to be honest with you, I'm heartily sick and tired of the whole thing. Having said that, though, it would be a shame if someone took it all over now and destroyed it. It would be a waste of so many years of effort. And it would be very easy to destroy it.'

'All you'd need to do would be to let them fight for that bone you mentioned, wouldn't it?'

'Yes. But I've got an advantage over them: I don't want any of it. I really don't. I've had enough. If you've never tasted that bread, you can't imagine how sour it is. Holy Mother, it is so very sour ... Only sour to those who do things honestly and want to serve people properly, of course. Because the man who's got some other harebrained aims, like he wants to be acclaimed by the masses, for example, or he wants power – well, naturally, he'll fight to get them and he won't give them up when he's got them. But an honest man tires of it all very quickly. It's just too hard.'

'How will Solidarity stop the central leadership becoming alienated from the grass roots? How will it stop the union from splitting into "them" and "us"?'

'There'll be no splits while I'm here.'

'None of the Western trade unions have managed to prevent the split. What guarantees can you give?'

'I'll go round the stadiums. At least once every year I'll visit, personally, every large region. And when I'm there we'll be able to say what we have to say to each other – face to face. Besides that, we'll introduce a system of questionnaires. All the works will conduct surveys as often as once a month, if necessary. People will be issued with sheets of paper headed with the words: "Write down what you would like to see done, what complaints you have, against whom" and so on. But that's not all. There's 16 December. That's my day. Because I was the one who was instrumental in putting that monument up. I sat in gaol longer than anyone else to get it. And

---

* Stanisław Kania replaced Edward Gierek as Party leader in September 1980, in the wake of the agreements signed at Gdańsk, Szczecin and Jastrzębie. He was not able to overcome the paralysis of the state and Party or to stem the advance of Solidarity, and in October 1981, when he had lost the confidence both of the Soviet leadership and most of his colleagues, he was replaced by General Jaruzelski.

every man, woman and child in Poland will know – write this down – that every year, on 16 December, I will be at that monument. Even if they isolate me completely ... There is no power on earth that will stop me doing that. And there, under that monument, we'll rehearse all we have to say to each other. And it will be there, if the need arises, that we'll set up free unions once again.'

'Do people still talk to you in the same way they did a year ago?'

'No, unfortunately, they don't. I notice it most when I drop in at the shipyard to see my old colleagues in the section. You'd need to change a lot of things in our Polish mentalities ... But that's a long-term process. It'd take generations.'

'Are you strong enough to continue being your own man, not allowing yourself to be bamboozled by anyone, not letting anyone set you up?'

'I am strong enough to be myself always and not to be set up by anyone – not my wife, not my children, not anyone.'

'How much of the day-to-day running of the union do you have to look after yourself?'

'I'm delegating more and more of my work to others. It wouldn't be possible for me to deal with everything. For example, I don't have as much to do with the running of the Gdańsk MKZ (Inter-works Founding Committee) as I used to. Zdzisław Złotowski does that for me. And I'm pushing new people into the talks with the government. The government has worked me out, psychologically speaking. They know how to play against me. So it's better if I send someone else in. Let them try to work him out. It gives them an extra problem to solve.'

'What do you think is the union's greatest achievement since August?'

'The fact that it exists.'

'What's your view on re-negotiations?'

'680 times 500. At this precise moment that is the number of points that still have to be put into practice, points that have already been agreed and signed. We have to reduce that lot to a total of two hundred, three hundred at most, and get down seriously to putting them into practice. And how do we do that? Very simply, and using the full majesty of our legislative bodies. Our representatives, our Members of Parliament and councillors, will do it for us. First of all, the KKP (National Co-ordinating Committee) will convene and distribute a hundred initial demands to each of the MKZs. The MKZs will then arrange meetings in the regions with their representatives. They'll give each one of them an identical package of demands – the same package of demands in Kraków, Bydgoszcz, Poznań – everywhere. The Members of Parliament will take the package with them to a session of the Sejm. There, cameras will be placed throughout the chamber so that they show clearly how each member votes. After the session, the Members of Parliament will return to the MKZs and give an account of their activities. That way it won't be us doing the hard work, it will be our representatives. Meanwhile we have to arrange meetings, hold discussions and explain why it is these particular points and not any others that are being given priority in the Sejm – and so on. That way we do the grass-roots work, and our representatives do the work at the top. And everything's under control.'

'The word "strike" doesn't seem to crop up as often as it did in your arguments. Why is that?'

'The strike, in its present form, belongs to the nineteenth and twentieth centuries. And we have to get rid of that kind of strike. Be sure you write that down. We must think of some alternative. I've got an idea; it's not something I'd insist on, mind. It's just a starting point for further discussion. People should try to come up with other solutions. My idea is this: Instead of stopping work when we strike, which only drives the country to ruin, we should strike by increasing productivity and then requisitioning the goods we produce for our own needs. Let's say we've announced a warning strike. Before we go ahead, we have talks with pensioners and orphanages, and we find out how many cars they need. And then, all the cars that are manufactured during the strike are handed over to people free of charge. We work only for ourselves, you see; we don't give the government anything. That way the country loses nothing, there is no waste, and we work better to provide for the neediest sectors of society. Enriching our country at the same time. The thing is that we mustn't destroy anything. Or take another example: We mine the coal, and then, instead of having it shipped to the ports, our cars take it straight from the collieries to the rural co-operatives to help the farmers.'

'The idea looks very noble, but it does seem a little far-fetched, doesn't it?'

'All right, think of something better. Look, I want people to be happy, and to have things. And they won't have things if they don't make them. So why shouldn't we make things and have them as well? Why shouldn't we be better off without all those who govern badly, or flout the law, or don't stick to agreements? Let's show them that we can manage on our own without damaging the economy. And, apart from the strike, the union's other major task is to put a brake on political activities. Anyone who forms any kind of political grouping is, effectively, dismantling the union.'

'But surely that's just an invention of official propaganda. You don't take the accusations about the union's "aggressive political activity" seriously, do you? That's just an excuse, a scaffold they're building so they can hang you. And an alibi for the person who does the hanging . . .'

'I agree. Nevertheless efforts are being made up and down the country which are aimed at setting up political parties. We don't need them. Instead of parties we should set up twenty trade unions. After all, the union in its present form will break up eventually.'

'You're right, but shouldn't we wait a few more years before we start putting that into operation? Right now don't we still need the strength of a ten-million-strong association, if only as a bargaining counter in discussions?'

'That goes without saying. But in a couple of years' time, there will have to be fifteen unions, not one. If I were a general, I'd demob five divisions and employ the biggest radicals and agitators in various plants. After a while we'd have nothing but majors in the KKP. These prospective fifteen unions would have to stick together on the most crucial questions, but in all other matters they'd be quite independent of each other. They'd have their own presses – and they could call each other names, revile each other and get rid of all that venom there's too much of in this union at present. But before that happens we'll get a joint agreement. The same agreement for everyone. A truly socialist agreement. Things can't go on the way they are at present with railwaymen getting free travel and me not getting it because I don't work on the railways. Miners dig the coal, so they'll get an extra ton of coal each – what's socialist about that? I can't be a miner if, for example, I make sausages . . . The distribution of the common good must be based on equality and justice.'

'Well, you've finally let something out, at the very end of our interview. You really do have a vision, a more panoramic view of the future. But won't you have to be careful not to put too much emphasis on equal shares for everyone? Equal shares isn't always the same as justice ... For example, you and your family are now, surely, less at the mercy of market shortcomings. You don't have to face the necessity of standing in queues, and so on.'

'I'm lucky in that people bring the things my children need round to our home. Yes, it's true I don't stand in queues. But I do see them. I sometimes ask myself: Why do people stand so patiently? I mean, obviously, it's not because they enjoy it. It must be because they're afraid.'

'Are they really afraid? Or is it simply that they understand the harsh realities?'

'You can understand things like that for a week, a fortnight, or even a month ... But it's been going on a bit too long and the queues are getting longer and longer ... So they must be affected by this neurotic fear where people know they've reached a breaking point, where they can't keep rebelling because, if they do, something will snap.'

'Do you really think so?'

'This is a very dangerous period we're in. I mean the last few months and years. Certain astonishing phenomena have appeared in the world, and they all have some kind of common denominator. A Polish Pope, Solidarity, a new president in the USA, a new president in France – nobody could have foreseen a combination of forces like that. There's a certain freshness in the world, and a lot of good hope. But what will happen if this hope proved to be false? If this new movement, scattered as it is over the whole world, proves incapable of converging and creating new forces – there'll be chaos, confusion and confrontation. That's what I'm frightened of most.'

'Do you believe that there is more good in people, or evil?'

'I believe there is more good in them, but we don't work hard enough at the most basic human qualities.'

'Is that where goodness is to be found – in simplicity?'

'In fundamental values, yes. We must remind ourselves what the simplest and most basic words mean – words like honesty and truth. We have too many complicated pieces of apparatus, machinery, computers, and we're trying to outsmart life with their help. All we think about is how to get on best, and how to get more for ourselves. We've gone too far in that direction. We've lost our sense of balance.'

'Thank you very much ... We don't want to go too far over the seven minutes you've allowed us ...'

'I've talked too much. You tricked me into this interview.'

'Thank you very much. We wish you luck.'

'Thank you both.'